Key Concepts in
Education

The SAGE Key Concepts series provides students with accessible and authoritative knowledge of the essential topics in a variety of disciplines. Cross-referenced throughout, the format encourages critical evaluation through understanding. Written by experienced and respected academics, the books are indispensable study aids and guides to comprehension.

FRED INGLIS AND LESLEY AERS

Key Concepts in
Education

SAGE

Los Angeles • London • New Delhi • Singapore • Washington DC

© Fred Inglis and Lesley Aers 2008

First published 2008

Apart from any fair dealing for the purposes of research or
private study, or criticism or review, as permitted under the
Copyright, Designs and Patents Act, 1988, this publication
may be reproduced, stored or transmitted in any form, or by
any means, only with the prior permission in writing of the
publishers, or in the case of reprographic reproduction, in
accordance with the terms of licences issued by the Copyright
Licensing Agency. Enquiries concerning reproduction outside
those terms should be sent to the publishers.

SAGE Publications Ltd
1 Oliver's Yard
55 City Road
London EC1Y 1SP

SAGE Publications Inc.
2455 Teller Road
Thousand Oaks, California 91320

SAGE Publications India Pvt Ltd
B 1/I 1 Mohan Cooperative Industrial Area
Mathura Road, New Delhi 110 044

SAGE Publications Asia-Pacific Pte Ltd
33 Pekin Street #02-01
Far East Square
Singapore 048763

Library of Congress Control Number: 2008924063

British Library Cataloguing in Publication data

A catalogue record for this book is available from the
British Library

ISBN 978-1-4129-0314-1
ISBN 978-1-4129-0315-8 (pbk)

Typeset by C&M Digitals (P) Ltd., Chennai, India
Printed in Great Britain by The Cromwell Press Ltd, Trowbridge, Wiltshire
Printed on paper from sustainable resources

contents

contents

v

key concepts in
education

contents

vii

How to use this book to help you think

... about teaching primarily, and about life as well. The book is entitled *Key Concepts* and as the relevant entry declares, a concept is an organising idea which serves to pick out certain features in an object of thought and distinguish it from other objects. It is therefore an instrument of thought. The greatest philosopher of his day, Ludwig Wittgenstein, writing in the 1940s, sets out many of the guiding principles which direct the definitions in this book.

He begins by insisting that the meaning of words is found in their many *uses*.

> Think of the tools in a toolbox: there is a hammer, pliers, a saw, a screwdriver, a rule, a glue-pot, glue, nails and screws. The functions of words are as diverse as the functions of these objects. (And in both cases there are similarities.) Of course, what confuses us is the uniform appearance of words when we hear them spoken or meet them in script or print. For their *application* is not presented to us so clearly.[1]

Wittgenstein goes on to say that we only understand the concepts we use as they assume their order in what he calls our 'language games', a phrase which he intends as bringing into prominence 'the fact that the *speaking* of language is part ... of a form of life'. This latter phrase is of the first importance, for it indicates that the meanings of concepts, which (as he says) are born, change, and die, and are replaced by new ones as our way of seeing experience is changed by our history, these meanings take their life from a whole shared context of continuing conversation. Education is one such form of life, and has its own multiplicity of language games. Wittgenstein continues,[2]

> Consider ... the proceedings we call 'games'. I mean board-games, card-games, ball-games, Olympic games and so on. What is common to them all? Don't say: 'There *must* be something common or they would not be called 'games', but *look and see* where there is anything common to all.

He then concludes that games are characterised by similarities which crop up and disappear, and that these 'family resemblances' are what mark out games as games, and similarly mark out different 'language games' with their various rules, conventions, ends and purposes. So too

> we extend [a] concept … as in spinning a thread we twist fibre on fibre. And the strength of the thread does not reside in the fact that some one thread runs through its whole length, but in the overlapping of many fibres.[3]

The language game of education is universally played; everybody has been to school, many people have children at school, the language game turns up all the time in newspapers, on radio and television. It offers a supreme example of a topic which may be and very often is discussed only in terms of prejudice, superstition, bigotry and ignorance, while nonetheless it is a language game which admits of proper rules of evidence, due respect for cited authority, rational disposition of argument and judgement. It implies, in other words, the conditions of ideal communication, the ideal end-result of which is that the best argument wins. Yet the terrific energy and ardour which typically enter into the language game of education suggest that for all the fact that some arguments are better than others, the subject itself – like art or marriage or the good life (all of them matters taken in by education) – can't be left alone. Our deepest allegiances – to identity, ethics, social status, career, to our parents and our children – are caught up in it. So we describe, analyse, complain, evaluate; we construct little household theories of educability, intelligence, creativity, learning (and its difficulties), genius, deserts. We talk of education for life, as a social system, as a set of structures, as a machinery, as a natural environment with horizons like a geography, as a natural process with flowers like horticulture, as a politics, as a torment and as a prison sentence. It is a prime number in the conversation of a culture, and inexhaustible.

So a little volume listing its key concepts, offering definitions – or better, offering their different uses – and attaching potted histories of those keys which might unlock their meanings, is a bold thing to compile. If it is not to invite error and crass simplification, this opening guide needs at once to break up the very notion of a 'list' which a lexicon must display.

For concepts do not come along to our cognitive apprehension one at a time. Indeed, it was the philosopher Kant, in the 1770s, who concluded that the human mind does not 'apprehend' concepts at all, but rather starts out *innately* equipped with at least the basic set it needs to begin to move through and render intelligible the world as it is. Such concepts form themselves necessarily into what the professionals (philosophers, psychologists, those people) call a conceptual scheme.[4]

They claim[5] – how could one disagree? – that for language to happen, for neural messages to the right part of the cortex to issue as sound, something conceptual has to be innate. This is less miraculous than it sounds. The 'something conceptual' cannot be culture-specific, but must be capable of sorting these necessities of conceptualisation into an intelligible order: event (the very idea of something happening), thing (what's this thing, this object?), path (where do I go?), place (where am I?), manner (how do I do this?), acting (what shall I do?), having (what have I got?) and so on, followed by a rush of concepts coming with an easy-to-comprehend urgency: living (or dead?), hard and soft, safe or dangerous, past, present, future (what is a memory?), means, goals, causing an event, or stopping it.

The eager reader might care to extend this list to the point at which culture intervenes and concepts need learning and do not arrive innately. The higher animals might be said to possess a number of the innate concepts, but the point at which innateness pushes its way into speech is held to be the point at which one crosses from the animal to the human kingdom.

This is not to say (a point we repeat in the entries on thinking and on concept) that a concept is necessarily attached to a word. Words name (or express) concepts; they don't create them. But the concept has no purchase on the world, cannot find its place in a conceptual scheme without the escort of language showing it the way to go. This is the point of our warning against conceptual *lists*; concepts announce their significance to the human mind by being fitted into the relevant place in the scheme or framework the mind uses for thought. But then the metaphor 'framework' (or structure) is not mobile enough to catch thought in *action*. Rather let us say that a conceptual scheme arranges itself in a dynamic order, the concepts enfolding or comprehending the experience or problem to hand, each playing off one against the other its particular usefulness in relation to the matter in hand.

Any attempt to picture this process must have recourse to metaphor, and there will be more to say about metaphor as the means by which new concepts find their way into the language in a moment. For now, however, we are imagining the play of a conceptual scheme upon an experience: a good teacher, perhaps, conducting a well-planned lesson before her only-average, clothes-obsessed, intermittently raucous, amiable-enough class of 25 daffy 14-year-olds.

When our teacher is thinking well, there is a heat in her concentration and a drive in her organisation quite beyond conscious control. Let us compare her to a good tennis player playing a hard match. Think of all the simultaneously coordinated movements the tennis player is making, the judgements as to the pace, movement, angle, feasibility of shot, and the effort and smoothness which must go into making it, and making it moreover not simply a winning shot, but a beautiful one also, as well-made as such a shot can be according to the conventions of the game. This is what it is like to apply the conceptual scheme summoned up for the purpose not just as best as one can make, but at the height of one's powers, and then at the height of the powers of someone really good at the job.

Then, if you are lucky, you will see the *art* of teaching in action – the art because the practice in question is being displayed with force and complexity, the life of the classroom is being directed with an assurance and subtlety intrinsic to art, the shape of the interior life of the lesson is made beautiful by the quiet animation of its participants, the smooth motion of their study from point to point, and all this lovely life advances to its goal, which is to discover the truthfulness for which class and teacher have set themselves to look.

Nobody talks about teaching like that these days. They never did, very much, in the past. But the predominance of what is called in these pages 'technicism', which is to say the supposition that teaching may be made foolproof by devising *impersonal* techniques and so-called 'skills' to cover all classroom and curricular life, has led to the treatment of all teachers as fools: creatures to be told what to do and never to be left alone to do it.

It isn't working. It'll go away. The aim of this book is to help dispel the inanities of technicism, the terrible tripe talked in the diction of the management of performance. The faith in this book is placed in certain inherent and indestructible attributes of the human mind which, when awoken, repel cant, mock jargon, deride cliché. These cheerfully oppositional forms of action are what one looks to find (ha!) in university departments of education. The key concepts are those which may so be orchestrated that they work on behalf of some of their best qualities – truth and beauty say; knowledge and freedom; equality and mind.

To be a teacher is to have the duty and be set the task in society of pointing out to the next generation the paths which lead forward out of the past and, by way of the always evanescent present, into a future to be made as safe as a parent would want to make it for the children while knowing that it is sure to be bloody dangerous.

There could hardly be anything more important for a person to do, could there? How is it, then, that schoolteaching has become not so much belittled, as ignored? Presumably the tendency is part of a widespread thinning out of the concept of authority. All authority figures agree (as people will) in being sorry for themselves that they don't command the respect they once had. Doctors say so, policemen say so, politicians aren't quite allowed to say so for fear of calling down still more recrimination on their heads than they do already, but they all think it. The political class, indeed, shares its predicament with teachers. Its function is to maintain social order, to burnish the best values of the day, to guard and ensure the emergence of a decent future out of a mixed past. But politicians, most of them worthy, honest, limited and well-meaning, are universally denigrated as self-seeking, power-mad, duplicitous and corrupt. By comparison, teachers get off lightly.

This unhappy state of affairs flows in part, for sure, from the loss of a shared vocabulary for the principles of public life. The radical individualisation of our lives over the past half-century, the enormous happiness brought by increased prosperity, by the freedoms of the happy self-indulgences of consumer life, the sumptuous goods, the sunny holidays, all this has eroded the powerful connections of community and class. To say so is an arrant truism, true for all that. So appeals to the common good have no very clear and solid application for their audience. And yet it is the duty of a schoolteacher to make those appeals and to speak, so far as he or she can, what the great poet, W. H. Auden, called 'a sane, affirmative speech'. The language of schoolteachers should make easy and practical reference to the best values of the day, as carried in the ordinary domestic exchanges of classroom, staffroom, school corridor, playground, assembly hall.

Is it to sound preachy to speak like this? Is the preacher standing in an empty church? For make no mistake; this book intends a kind of sermon, or better, a call to the colours. These, we believe, are key concepts because they may be selected from and ordered as instruments of thought, of teaching and learning, turned to the purposes of creating a better life in the classroom and ultimately a better life outside it.

Perhaps now is an inauspicious time to remind teachers of such a language. Yet this inauspiciousness is itself a token of urgency. One could say that the present is an historical moment of a kind which has several precedents in the past. One such example is offered by the Reformation in Christian belief whereby between the early 1500s and the end of the seventeenth century, the power of the Catholic Church was opposed by the new heresies of Martin Luther and John Calvin and many others, the empire of Catholicism shrank back into Spain and southern Italy, and the popular narratives of life and death, of monarch and people, became uncertain, contested, fragmentary, and at times hysterical with rage or of deathly indifference.

The present world circulates its narratives unbelievably faster, and new narratives of how to live pour out of crazy blogs as well as out of the official media and government or from church spokespeople. But ours is a moment like the Reformation, in that there is no one agreed-upon narrative for the transitions of everyday life; for commemorating the death of parents or consecrating the birth of infants; for sharing out the rewards and products of society; for facing the terrible menace of a natural world which has always seemed to look after us, and now faces us as though it were become the Hindu god, Vishnu, destroyer of worlds.

No one lives ordinary life at this pitch, or not without losing their mental and moral balance. Perhaps, however, if this brief description of our historical moment is right, it is no wonder that teachers aren't sure what to say about the old joke, the meaning of life, nor that their pupils don't want to listen very hard, and would rather leave tomorrow to look after itself, and to hide in the aisles of the glittering malls.

Insofar as teachers must do what they can – they have their professional duties and sometimes, it is to be hoped, their vocation, then doing what they can will be done by way of the concepts which follow. But a concept has no intellectual content of its own; it cannot tell you what to do. It is a tool of thought, an instrument with which to make the world intelligible and action in the world effective. Application of the concept is all in the hands and minds and hearts of individuals, and therefore of the society which is product of their joint efforts and labour. It is not that our key concepts carry no charge of value or of historical accretion: to carry value and the weight of human experience are what our concepts are *for*. But that value and weight are only discharged into action, for better or worse, by the use to which a person puts them.

That person uses the concept well when she follows the rules for using it correctly. But she has to use it for herself, and in that use, insofar as her use is creative (insofar, that is, as she invents new metaphors to think with), the concept gathers up tiny new charges for the advantage of those who pick it up thereafter.[6] Certainly, the individual concept has a structure of its own, compounded of the rules for understanding its 'sense' and then, by using it, giving it 'reference'. But the grander significance of a primer of 'key concepts' is that each of these which follow occupies a position in upholding complete social philosophies.

Thus, it is that to use 'equality' (one of the teacher's and the society's most important words) is to balance it against 'liberty', 'justice', 'individual', 'society' and so forth. It simply cannot be isolated by itself. To say this is to offer this whole book to present and future teachers, for passing reference of course, but also as a cartographic kit, the essential instruments from which those teachers may make a map of their world: paths and landmarks; mountain ranges and marshlands; limits and frontiers; and somewhere, in the most beautiful stretch of countryside, the good city, the city of reason, where the promise of happiness will be kept and to which all educational artists and craftspeople may come safely home.

NOTES

1 Ludwig Wittgenstein (1953), *Philosophical Investigation*, Oxford: Basil Blackwell, para 11.
2 Ibid., para 66.
3 Ibid., para 67.
4 Donald Davidson (1980), 'On the very idea of a conceptual scheme', in *Actions and Events*, Oxford: Oxford University Press.
5 Steven Pinker (2007), *The Stuff of Thought: Language as a Window into Human Nature*, New York: Viking.
6 Much is taken here from Quentin Skinner's (2002) essay on the meaning and use of concepts 'The idea of a cultural lexicon', in his *Visions of Politics*, vol 1, Cambridge: Cambridge University Press.

How to use this book in general

You may need to look up a single reference, or you may want to read several related ones together. In every entry, there are cross-references: a word that is covered in the book as one of the 'concepts' is written in bold, almost invariably the first time it is used in the entry. You will also find, at the end of almost all the entries, a short bibliography (books and some websites), that will enable you to explore the concept in greater depth. Many entries give a wide, historical view of the concept under scrutiny; in others, where the word has acquired a specific meaning in current educational usage, this meaning is explained as precisely as possible.

Like **potential**, 'ability' is a slippery term, and an individual's ability is, in itself, impossible to measure. Attainment can be measured through various forms of testing, which provide evidence of a specific kind of ability, demonstrated under particular circumstances. These results are used by **schools** to project forward, and set **targets** for pupils, assuming that their 'ability' continues to develop smoothly.

Teachers themselves are well aware of the fact that the children they work with have a wide range of abilities. One of the problems they face is to ensure that their lessons are suitable for everyone, or, as the Ofsted framework puts it, '**work** is closely tailored to the full range of learners' needs, so that all can succeed'. Lesson plans are meant to show 'differentiation', which means varying the approaches, or the tasks set, so that these are suitable for all the children, from the highest to the lowest ability. Obviously, this is easier said than done. Larger schools often use **strategies** such as setting or **streaming** to try to limit the range of ability in a class. In a smaller school, this is impossible. For example, a single class in a small primary school might include children of different ages, as well as of widely differing ability.

Related terms are 'capability', which is as hard to pin down as ability, and also 'disability', which usually refers to a specific physical problem. Schools often use 'able' as a description, and may include a section in their lesson plans for 'MATs' – more able and talented pupils.

Tests have been devised which are meant to assess general ability, as the old IQ tests (**intelligence** quotient) were meant to do. The commercial 'Cognitive Abilities Test' (CATs) assess verbal, non-verbal and numerical reasoning. Whether these add anything to the results of national assessments is doubtful.

ability

9

Academy

The word 'academy' comes from the name of the garden near Athens where Plato taught. It now means a place of **learning**, including a **school**, although related words such as 'academic' or 'academe' tend to refer to university studies.

'Academy' is often used for a specialised institution, such as the French Academy in Paris, the Imperial Academy of St Petersburg, or London's Royal Academy of Painting, Sculpture and Architecture. When the word is applied to a school, it can carry a whiff of pretension, beautifully illustrated here by Dickens in *Nicholas Nickleby*:

> Education – At Mr Wackford Squeers's Academy, Dotheboys Hall, at the delightful village of Dotheboys, near Greta Bridge in Yorkshire. Youth are boarded, clothed, furnished with pocket-money, provided with all necessaries, instructed in all languages, living and dead, mathematics, orthography, geometry, astronomy, trigonometry, the use of the globes, algebra, single stick [fencing] (if required), writing, arithmetic, fortification, and every other branch of classical literature. Terms, twenty guineas per annum. No extras, no vacations, and diet unparalleled.

As we quickly find out, the ominous 'no vacations' meant that the school was a dumping ground for unwanted children, and the diet was indeed 'unparalleled' in its inadequacy.

How unlike our own academies. These were introduced by the Labour government, announced in 2000 by David Blunkett when he was secretary of state for education. They are lavishly funded, much more so than other state schools. The average cost for each of the first 12 was £23 million, and in others it was considerably higher. The other difference from mainstream schools in funding is that academies have to have a 'sponsor'. Sponsors could be 'businesses, **individuals**, churches and other faith groups, or voluntary bodies'. The sponsor was to provide £2 million of the total cost. Several of them have not, in the end, given that amount.

For their relatively small contribution, sponsors acquire almost absolute control of the school, as they are able to appoint a majority on the governing body. They can decide what is taught, as academies are exempt from the National **Curriculum**. They can determine pay scales and employment conditions. This is in spite of the fact that most of the costs are paid from public funds.

In the beginning, the project was that academies would replace failing schools, usually in inner-city areas. It is laudable that there should be extra funding and splendid new buildings for the poorest children, who in the past tended to get the worst facilities. However, academies are now replacing schools which may be successful or improving schools, not necessarily in inner cities.

There is considerable debate about the extent to which academies have raised **standards** so far. In some, results have improved above the schools which the academy replaced, although the intake is not exactly the same. Academies are attracting more middle-class parents, because of the new buildings and resources. There is no evidence that the results achieved by academies are due to their model of sponsorship and independence, rather than the extra funding they receive.

Academies are independent of the local **authority**, even though the LA has a **responsibility** to monitor schools within its area. The LA also has a duty to find places in its schools for pupils who are excluded, and up to now, academies have been chucking out a relatively high number. Nevertheless, a new shift in government policy allows LAs or universities to become sponsors. It will be interesting to see how this works, and how it will affect relationships between schools in the area, especially if the inequitable funding continues.

FURTHER READING

Francis Beckett (2007), *The Great City Academy Fraud*. London: Continuum.
Specialist Schools and Academies Trust: www.specialistschools.org.uk
www.standards.dcsf.gov.uk/academies

academy

As the big institutions of modern **society** have more and more come to organise our lives, a movement in social **democracy** has gathered pace which, recognising how little it is that **individuals** can do to control or criticise these creatures, seeks to transform their **authority** and **responsibility** into *accountability*. This means that systems of reckoning be devised which will regularly review performances, in particular of the state **bureaucracies** (**schools**, hospitals, welfare, benefits, pensions, police, etc.) and, in drawing up such audits, balance sheets, inspectorial reports and so on, will render up *accounts* – accounts which take in not just how the money has been spent (though that above all), but also whether, in the jargon, '**value** has been added', whether the institutions have made a difference, given value for money, met their **targets**, put on an adequate performance.

These are the key **concepts** of accountability, and they lock together in a powerful **structure** of surveillance. The nineteenth-century social reformer, Jeremy Bentham, imagined an ideal prison in which open walkways, fretted doors, glass walls and a huge watchtower would make it possible to observe, control and constrain the **behaviour** of inmates every moment of the day and night. He called this the Panopticon, and accountability systems have been likened to it.

If so, there is some unfairness to the comparison. Accountability is intended to make large institutions answerable to those they are supposed to serve. The French sociologist Durkheim pointed out that in a complex society with very elaborate divisions of labour and specialisation (the kind of society he called 'organicist'), the **principles** of social order could not be left implicit. They must be made explicit. Hence the slogan 'transparency' which decorates the procedures of accountability. The argument goes that if we can all see plainly how things work, we will know whom to blame when they don't.

This is where things begin to go wrong. As Onora O'Neill points out, the new accountability officers are well-armed, punitive and everywhere. Performance is, in the phrase, monitored and subjected to **quality** controls and assurance: a university or a school course has its quality assessor, is marked fit for consumption, and given a sell-by date just like a piece of Camembert. The very idea of an *audit* has been borrowed from the finance officer and stretched to cover ever more detailed analysis and reports of (in teaching establishments) marketing, consumer (that is, student) satisfaction, obsolescence, relevance and the rest.

One result has been the creation of a quite new social fraction, made up of such inspectors, assessors, cost-benefit analysts and quality controllers. As must always be the case, such people are much resented and feared by those they come to inspect, as well as mistrusted as not actually doing the work of those they come to hold accountable.

The result is much less a vindication of public trust than an intensification of mistrust, and a steady diminution of personal commitment in the activity under audit. Where a teacher (or a nurse, or a social worker, or a counsellor) is minutely and too regularly checked for performance and assessed against external criteria for every step in the lesson, the job is emptied of personal or inner meaning and the **art** of teaching or nursing or counselling is destroyed. This is one fearful consequence of what is elsewhere in this book named 'technicism': the drive to make all workers, but especially those in the public welfare institutions, substitutable, to turn the arts of attention to and care for others into **techniques**, so to monitor human oddity that it is squeezed out by efficiency. **Standards** are set explicitly and from outside; institutions are publicly ranked from top to bottom; schools, hospitals and university departments are liable to closure if they are too small, or their numbers fall, or their productivity drops.

Time and again the external criteria of **assessment** are incoherent. The drive to meet the most important targets means that other targets are missed; in schools, targeting itself, on for example **literacy** and numeracy, leads to a thinning out in the broader educational realm. Accountability, however well-intentioned, has done much to damage the social value of trust. The problem remains how to hold the connections between the **vocations** of care, the acquisition of the specialised **knowledge** necessary to the practitioner of care, the human need for personal contact and affection, and the essential maintenance of high standards. The answer lies somewhere in the tensions between accountability and responsibility, trust and evaluation.

accountability

FURTHER READING

Robin Alexander (2007), *Primary Education in England*. Cambridge: Cambridge University Press.

J. L. Austin (1961), 'A plea for excuses', *Philosophical Papers*. Oxford: Oxford University Press.

Onora O'Neill (2002), *A Question of Trust*. Cambridge: Cambridge University Press.

Michael Comer (1997) *The Audit Society*. Oxford: Oxford University Press.

Andreas Schedler, Larry Diamond and Mark F. Plattners (eds) (1991), *The Self-Restraining State: Power and Accountability in Democracies*. London: Riener.

'Achievement' can have a large, vague meaning, such as 'the sum total of human **experience**'. However, the word has come to have a precise meaning in current educational terminology. At one time, modest goals could be achieved. A teacher could say, 'He needed a grade C, and he achieved that,' irrespective of whether this was the highest grade the pupil was capable of or not.

Achievement is now judged against the prediction. If the pupil was expected to get a C, and he got a C, that is satisfactory achievement. If he got a B, that is good achievement; an A or A* would be outstanding. If he was expected to get a B, and got a C, that is judged as under-achievement. Predictions are set according to a pupil's prior attainment. Good achievement means that the pupil has made good **progress**.

Achievement should not be confused with **standards**. Standards are fixed according to national averages. Thus, one **school** can have its standards described as good, because they are above the national average, but achievement might be only satisfactory (or even unsatisfactory) if the prior attainment of pupils shows that results should have been better. The school down the road might have exactly the same standards, but achievement is good if they have done better than was expected. The school is said to have 'added **value**'.

Nowadays, schools monitor their pupils' achievements according to regular **assessments**, not just final **examinations**. If a pupil is not progressing steadily towards the predicted grade, he or she will be described as 'underachieving' and will be the subject of extra **attention**, such as mentoring or booster sessions. There is no hiding place now for the pupil who just 'needs a C' and doesn't want to work any harder in order to get a higher grade.

key concepts in education

Arts

The arts now gather under that very general heading all those practices designated 'expressive' or, sometimes, 'imaginative', and conventionally include painting, sculpture, music (composition and performance), drama (ditto), all forms of written literature (poetry, novels and so forth), and dance. To this traditional list there has been added, over the past century, photography, film, computer graphics (at a pinch) and, in some arguments, sport, chess and even card games.

To make arguments about the intrinsic nature of art (as opposed to the catch-all title, 'the arts') an insistence on definition is usually a sterile exercise. What has been called (by Herbert Hart) 'the definitional stop' is rarely as satisfactory a move in demonstrating what art really is as pointing to examples and saying 'there it is'. Pointing at or listening to such unmistakable works of great art as Botticelli's *Birth of Venus*, Mozart's *Jupiter* symphony, Shakespeare's *Macbeth* or Rossellini's movie *Paesa* is of course initially convincing because of the strength of the **experience** of each. But then one is bound to ask what they have in common which makes them conceptually alike, and that is the point at which fierce fighting breaks out.

At this point it is important to distinguish between art and craft, and to say that while craft is the application of a **technique** to the production of a specific end, art is the process whereby one accomplishes an end which one could not envisage to begin with. The end which is the **work** of art is an answer to a **question** one has set oneself without being able to foresee what an answer would look like.

This, however, is only the beginning. The same thing could be said about a new mathematical theorem or an inquiry into biogenetics. What makes a work of art just that is also its expressive power, its imaginative force, its shapely **beauty**, its **truth** to experience, its intellectual seriousness, or at least enough of some of these to qualify it as work of good art (and not bad).

All these **qualities** can only be found ostensively, that is to say, by being shown them in action. The greatest of all novelists, Leo Tolstoy, said that any well-told tale in a conversation which made the listener feel what the narrator wanted to make him or her feel was thereby a work of art, but this won't really do because one can't simply *transfer* a set of feelings from person to person. Rather, one can say that the work of art is accomplished when one is able to express emotions of one's own about it by means of the artist's realisation – whether in words or paint or music.

On the way to this expression or realisation all kinds of things may go wrong. Bad art, R. G. Collingwood tells us, is the kind of art which deceives us about our own feelings, which makes us (in D. H. Lawrence's words) 'work off on ourselves feelings we haven't really got'. Magic art, a subcategory, is, on the contrary, the art we use to work *up* certain feelings in order to discharge them into action. Military music is one example of this, the drama of the political rally another.

Good art, however, is found when thought and feeling are held perfectly at poise in the form the artist has created for them. There can be no technique for such accuracy of expression. Our consciousness is corrupt (in Collingwood's phrase) whenever we seek to satisfy the duty to self-**knowledge** by technical, that is, ready-made and procedural means (some therapists are guilty of this; all soaps are; most crime thrillers are). The point of art and therefore of *the* arts, is to discover clarity, richness and purity of expression. Such discoveries are **individual** and particular. They may be glad or painful but, as the novelist Stendhal wrote, reassuringly, 'art holds out the promise of happiness'.

FURTHER READING

Malcolm Budd (1995), *Values of Art*. Harmondsworth: Penguin.
R. G. Collingwood (1938), *The Principles of Art*. Oxford: Oxford University Press.
Ken Robinson (1996), *The Arts in Schools, Principles, Practice and Provision*. London: Callouste Gulbenkian.
Leo Tolstoy (1975), *What is Art?* Oxford: World's Classic Editions.

key concepts in education

Assessment

Assessment, in educational terms, covers a range of different processes. Traditionally, it meant assessment at the end of a year or a course, usually by formal timed **examinations**. 'Exams' require a particular **skill** of writing to the clock, and some teachers and lecturers questioned whether this was the best mode of assessment. A **method** was sought which might cover a wider range of skills, and this led to various kinds of 'continuous assessment'.

In the 1960s, the Joint Matriculation Board developed a continuously assessed O Level English Language qualification which had no timed exam at all. Across the two years of the course, students produced 10 pieces of **work**, demonstrating different reading and writing skills. Students were able to prepare in their own time, although the actual piece of work was written under controlled conditions. Teachers marked the work, and attended moderation meetings with the board. A leading article in the *Daily Telegraph* at the time criticised this new type of examination as one which 'too many people would pass'.

Continuous assessment led to the notion of coursework, which is usually prepared and produced in the students' own time. It is marked by teachers and a sample is moderated by the exam board. It is under attack at the moment because of the difficulty of knowing whether students have either had help from their parents, or have copied some sections from other essays, perhaps on the internet, rather than doing all the work themselves.

Coursework tends to be written but there are also examples of 'oral assignments' when students take part in a discussion, or give a presentation, which is assessed as part of the course. This is necessarily transitory, and evidence is provided by the teacher's notes on the session. Some of these assignments are moderated by an examiner.

Some students prefer the old-style formal examination, as they feel that continuous assessment puts them under pressure to perform well all the time, rather than at the end of the course. There is also an argument that assessment at the end makes more sense, as that is when the student should be at his or her most well-informed, and with the most fully developed skills. Some courses are now 'modular' which means they are divided into chunks, or modules, and each chunk is assessed separately.

With the introduction of GCSEs in the 1980s, assessments for schools, as organised by the examination boards, moved away from being 'norm-referenced' to being 'criterion-referenced'. 'Norm-referencing' assumed that cohorts were roughly the same year on year, so the same percentage would pass or fail (or get A grades). The pass mark was adjusted accordingly. This overcame the problem of exams not being standardised – that is, different papers and questions are set each year.

When assessments became 'criterion-referenced', it meant that students would be assessed against specific criteria, and whoever met the criteria would pass (and get the relevant grade). Courses are now planned around the 'assessment criteria' which are clearly stated in the syllabus. Not surprisingly, a higher percentage of students now passes, and reaches higher grades. This causes consternation in some quarters, just as it did in the *Daily Telegraph* in the 1960s.

Assessment is not just used to give a grade at the end of a course or a Key Stage (and pupils in English schools – but not Welsh or Scottish – have more of this kind of assessment than pupils anywhere else). Teachers use 'formative assessment', which is assessment made during a course to help pupils improve. This is not to put pressure on pupils; it is to support them. The quality of the feedback is crucial. Teachers put a comment on the work to identify what has been done well, and then give guidance on how to make an improvement. The advice has to have a precise enough focus to make a difference. For example, 'improve your spelling' does not help very much.

This type of assessment is also called 'assessment for learning', and pupils are involved as much as possible. For a particular assignment, criteria are made clear to pupils, and then when the work is completed they can engage in self-assessment. Pupils also work in partnership on 'peer-assessment', to check whether all the criteria have been met.

FURTHER READING

Patricia Broadfoot (1996), *An Introduction to Assessment*. London: Continuum.
John Gardner (ed.) (2005), *Assessment and Learning*. London: Sage.
Wynne Harlen (2007), *Assessment of learning*. London: Sage.

key concepts in education

Attention

'Pay attention' the teacher says crossly, and the timeless, familiar phrase reminds us once more, just as the no less familiar phrase does, 'How are you spending your time?' that time is money, and that attention is a coin in the same currency. Being attentive is perhaps the opposite of the state of **boredom**, but it is difficult to determine whether one's attention is a feature of mind and character, or whether it is a cast of thought called up by the object of my attention.

For sure, teachers have learned from psychologists a fancy name – attention deficit disorder – with which to describe the sort of awful pupil who will turn to no task for more than a few seconds, runs unstoppably around the classroom in distraction and destruction of class order, is invariably resentful and high-pitched in opposition to doing any school **work**. The phrase, however, has no explanatory content; it simply names a condition, perhaps the consequence of chemical imbalance, checked only by the sort of sedation which removes personality.

There can be no doubt that habits of attention may be taught and learned, as well as brought to the desk by the nature of child or student. On the one hand, the **traditions** of a **subject** teach the right kind of attention; on the other, the thrill of the subject or the gifts of the teacher or the character of the student ('he's very focused', as people say) command the right kind of attention.

There are as many kinds of attention as there are modalities of **thinking**. You may be attentive while musing, ruminating, meditating, analysing, speculating, cogitating, watching, but you can't be attentive while daydreaming, star-gazing (in the slangy sense), drifting, wondering. Attention is lost, as the revealing phrase goes, when it wanders. Yet at times, wandering and wondering inattentively are exactly what the topic you are thinking about may demand. And the word has its ambiguities. To be standing to attention on parade is to be stiff with apprehension awaiting the next order but forced to a rigid immobility, staring fixedly to the front until commanded to move in strictly regulated movements. To attend in its weak sense means simply to turn up ('I attended the meeting'), but to attend *to* ('to be attent' is the archaic phrase now only found in poetry) is to give one's earnest regard to the matter in hand, and it is plain that whatever the disposition of a student, small children's powers of sustained attention are limited; they are constantly giving attention to the sheer multitudinousness of the delicious world, leaving one thing for another, and only acquiring the **discipline** of attention by refusing to attend to all the other things which fairly cry out for their attention.

Naturally, attention is more than simply looking hard, it is *selective* and intensely cognitive, which is to say that it is the product of seeking answers to **questions**. For attention to have point and purpose, it must be directed by question of identical point and purpose, exactly formulated and precisely answerable. As someone said, 'to ask questions you see no prospect of answering is the fundamental sin in science', and asking such questions is a consequence of inattention.

FURTHER READING

D. E. Broadbent (1958), *Perception and Communication*. Oxford: Pergamon.
Kenneth Burke (1945), *A Grammar of Motives*. New York: Prentice Hall.
Liam Hudson (1968), *Frames of Mind*. London: Jonathan Cape.
R. S. and C. H. Kempe (1978), *Child Abuse*. London: Fontana/Open Books.
David Wood (1990), *How Children Think and Learn*. Oxford: Basil Blackwell.

key concepts in education

Authority

Authority is the right to command. This immediately begs the **question** – who gives this **right**? Medieval kings believed it had been granted by God, and that they were God's deputies on earth. The authority of modern government has been conferred by the people (or at least, the ones who bother to vote) through the ballot box. Debate still rages, however, as to how far that authority should go, in interfering in people's lives.

Authority is questioned and sometimes treated with contempt, increasingly so in modern times. In order to be fully effective on its own terms, it has to have **power** to enforce obedience. In medieval times, questioning the king (or God) would get you hanged. Nowadays, obedience is enforced by the army or the police. They are highly evident in **societies** that are dictatorships, and punishments are harsh. In societies such as our own, the army is rarely evident (except, until recently, in Northern Ireland). The police are visible and have been known to misuse their power. The government uses its authority to pass laws, in order to shape the kind of society it wants, and the police have to enforce the laws. Some laws will limit the **freedom** of some **individuals**, for example the smoking ban, because the government believes this would be for the benefit of society as a whole. Police cannot question the law, although they might turn a blind eye on occasion. Some are more zealous than others.

Those who are in a position to enforce laws, such as soldiers, police, traffic wardens and the judiciary, have special uniforms, which are visible manifestation of their power. It should not matter who is inside the uniform, as they have the full back-up of the system. As King Lear says, 'a dog's obeyed in office'.

In the early years of the twentieth century, the German sociologist Max Weber discerned in modern society three types of authority and what he called 'imperative co-ordination'. His prime interest was in power, and authority is the ambient force or aura which permits the particular agent to exercise power. The last resort of power is violence, and only the state can administer legitimate violence.

Many people in authority (especially, perhaps, teachers) are sentimental about it. They don't want to see it exercised nakedly; they disclaim that they have it. But they should be clear about one political fact: law and order mean strength. Law and order are only upheld by whatever forces have the authority, and it is better for everyone if that authority is wielded by the officers of the state. Only if the state becomes tyrannical is it justified to challenge its authority, and when this happens the social order is in crisis anyway.

Of course, authority may be ascribed to somebody as a natural attribute; a very tall, imposing, perhaps good-looking person may be described as 'having authority', and someone very well-informed upon a particular subject may be described as 'an authority'. But our prime concern here is with that kind of social authority which compels obedience. There has to be such authority for society to function, and there is no doubt that teachers must embody it effectively, and teach respect for it as well.

This being so, Weber's three categories are useful for analysing authority in **school**. The first is traditional authority, whereby antique modes of power and **wisdom** lend authority to those figures endowed with such **qualities** by historical belief and custom. Kings, elders, patriarchs are the figures (mostly male) looming from our past with this kind of authority, and although it is nowadays much weakened, it is not finished.

The second of Weber's categories is 'charismatic' authority in which command is ceded to force of character, inspiring rhetoric, perhaps terrific 'presence' set off by impressive uniform and theatrical accoutrements (grand vehicles, loudspeakers, high platforms). Political dictators often possess charismatic authority and have, as Weber points out, a good deal of difficulty trying to turn it to everyday effectiveness and to make their charisma work 'routinely'. Charismatic authority may well be exercised by certain sorts of teacher, but only by keeping the students in a condition of continuous excitement.

The third kind of authority is the kind with which we are familiar as a product of modernity. It is 'legal-bureaucratic', established on the grounds of expediency and rational public **values**, and assented to as reasonable and necessary by the citizens. Those who wear its authority are 'officials' and they are bound by the strict and well-understood rules of their bureaucratic office.

The authority of teachers may partake of all three of Weber's types, but rests finally on the last.

Teachers do not have uniforms to symbolise their authority, and the back-up they get varies from school to school. Ultimately, if all the pupils decided to walk out of school together, nothing could be done to stop them; but in practice, there is always a majority which wants to toe the line.

State schools, except for academies, are within a local authority (LA). Until 2006, these were called local education authorities (LEAs); now they are called Children's Services Authorities. The internal organisation of a school is a matter for the governors, in conjunction with the head-teacher, until things go seriously wrong, when LAs have to take measures relating to schools 'causing concern'. The LA is the employer of staff in schools, although teachers are appointed by schools themselves (theoret-ically, by the governors). The only appointment that the LA has the right to attend is that of the headteacher, and the governors are not required to follow the LA's advice, although if the school later on 'causes concern', they would only have themselves to blame. Schools set their own admis-sions criteria, but the LA has the **responsibility** to ensure that all pupils have a place somewhere. If a school has spare places, a pupil cannot be refused. If a pupil is excluded from school, the LA has to find him or her a place, either in another school or in a 'pupil referral unit'.

Other statutory responsibilities of LAs include what is referred to as 'commissioning', which means working with other public bodies, private and voluntary organisations in order to get the best services for schools.

It can be seen from this that LAs no longer have much 'authority' in its original sense, but act as a back-up support service to ensure that their schools run as smoothly as possible – but schools can choose their mode of operation, as long as they follow the National Curriculum. Nevertheless, the LA will generally get blamed when something goes wrong.

LEAs were more authoritarian in the past, and still are in some other countries. For example in China, teachers do not apply to a specific school; the LEA directs staff according to the needs of particular schools. This ensures that the best schools do not just act as magnets to the best staff.

authority

FURTHER READING

Geoffrey Bantock (1963), *Freedom and Authority in Education*. London: Chatto and Windus.

John Dunn (2001), *The Cunning of Unreason: Making Sense of Politics*. London: HarperCollins.

Clifford Geertz (1983), 'Centres, Kings and Charisma' in *Local Knowledge*. New York: Basic Books.

Max Weber (1947), *The Theory of Social and Economic Organisation*, edited by Talcott Parsons. New York: Free Press.

Even if the word itself is not used, the **concept** is high on the list of the **qualities** which an **education** hopes to bestow upon its pupils. Autonomy translates into its two Greek components as 'the self' plus 'the law', and is counterposed to heteronomy which comes from 'others' plus 'law'. In other words, autonomy is that quality shown by someone who is self-possessed, self-controlled, self-propelling, self-reliant, all of them properties of a free **individual** as we hope they will emerge from our **schools**.

Once we start free-associating in this way, it is an easy matter to group beside autonomy other such **values** as **responsibility**, alongside the special emphasis given to the adjective 'personal' in our ethics (as in personal choice or personal values). This emphasis on personal autonomy (which is the figure of speech known as a *pleonasm*: autonomy can only be personal) and the powerful, associated value of *authenticity*, starts out from the terrific explosion placed under conventional **morality** and its educational precepts by the Romantic movement after about 1770. Romanticism taught not only the splendour of passionate feeling but also the excellence of self-expression, as well as the importance of both to the autonomous self. Kant was the philosopher of this movement, and he codified what poets such as Wordsworth and composers such as Beethoven expressed in their art.

Kant taught that the individual conscience is the last court of appeal, not 'heteronymous' law (the law of others). The appeal of this doctrine was strong and in the thought of J.-P. Sartre became the main precept of existentialism, a moral and political body of belief for which certain life-defining choices gave form and meaning to a life. This is now widely thought to be rather too melodramatic an account of the moral life, whereas people mostly puzzle out their **judgements** less finally than required in existentialism.

Nonetheless, autonomy is of undoubted presence in the ethics of education, where teachers encourage pupils to come to their own decisions, such as which **examinations** to take and **careers** to pursue. Probably the most memorable way to discuss the concept in a lesson is to ask pupils whether an autonomous individual, in full possession of his or her faculties, should be legally permitted to ask for euthanasia, and, furthermore, whether to refuse such a request is to violate that person's autonomy.

FURTHER READING

Gerald Dworkin (1988), *The Theory and Practice of Autonomy*. Cambridge: Cambridge University Press.
J.-P. Sartre (1969), *Being and Nothingness*. London: Methuen.
Lionel Trilling (1974), *Sincerity and Authenticity*. Oxford: Oxford University Press.
Mary Warnock (2000), *A Memoir*. London: Duckworth.

autonomy

On the face of it, beauty is a simple and enormously important **idea**. Neither its simplicity nor its importance should be obscured for a moment. For people readily say that someone or something – a baby, a view, a creature, a line of poetry, a melody, an action – is beautiful, and say so without affectation, but as naming something obvious and delightful.

So when aestheticians and educationists make, as they sometimes do, weary weather of the concept of beauty, we need to keep in mind the simple and accurate use of the word in everyday conversation. No doubt people also say that 'beauty is in the eye of the beholder', and there are indeed endless and absorbing arguments about whether something is beautiful or not. But there is also widespread agreement within particular **cultures** and **societies** as to what beauty is, agreement which spreads wider as cultural differences become less marked and exclusive. Non-Japanese students of art readily appreciate the paintings of Hokusai; Samoans and Maoris delight in Mozart.

Plato said that the beautiful is the one good which each of us can love immediately and naturally, and that it was so important not only in itself but as leading human beings on to love the other two **qualities** in his trinity, **truth** and goodness. Even if nowadays some reservation might be expressed about the directness of this connection, most theories of **teaching** as well as of the arts would place the **experience** of beauty near the centre of their concerns, and be pretty confident that pupils with a strong feeling for and a sure grasp of the nature and significance of beauty have a better chance of becoming decent and cultivated human beings than those who don't.

Nonetheless beauty is not necessarily just there to be apprehended. Edmund Burke made a distinction between the beautiful and the sublime, the latter being found in objects which break open traditional ideas of formal beauty by their awesome and overwhelming properties. Mighty storms, colossal mountain ranges, vast explosions, the heavens themselves, could be sublime in this category-destructive but uplifting way.

At this point, sublimity crosses into religious (or numinous) terrain, whereas beauty may be thought of as homelier and more familiar. When this is so, beauty becomes endangered by kitsch, which is to say beauty is made saccharine, its power and purity not just softened and sweetened but deprived of their truthfulness and grace, turned into a presence without mystery and a prettiness without strength. W. B. Yeats wrote in one poem of a 'terrible beauty' and while not all beauty need have terror as one of its effects, the **concept** of beauty always includes in its scope something tremendous, a revelation capable of shifting one's life a little somewhere, an untamable energy.

Beauty, then, must have both form and force. It cannot be applied to *anything*. That form will be at once right and surprising; the forcefulness will be creative of both fear and happiness.

FURTHER READING

John Armstrong (2004), *The Secret Power of Beauty.* London: Allen Lane.
M. Mothersill (1984), *Beauty Restored.* Oxford: Oxford University Press.
Alexander Nehamas (2007), *Only a Promise of Happiness: The Place of Beauty in a World of Art.* Princeton: Princeton University Press.

beauty

Like so many of the **concepts** in educational discourse, behaviour has a conversational and a technical meaning. In the conversation of staffrooms, behaviour is a synonym for the conduct of the pupils, and good and bad behaviours are no more than classifications of approval or disapproval by teachers of what their pupils did in the playground or on the **school trip**. The behaviour observed in school as a whole is one of the features to be judged during an **inspection**.

Round about the beginning of the twentieth century, however, psychology began to assert itself as another one of the human sciences with a claim to the crown of all the sciences. As a **discipline** (and a set of professional associations) it split into two, rivalrous and mutually censorious camps, one taking Freud's discoveries away to specialise in the study of the subconscious, the other, flourishing in the USA, rejecting the study of **mind** as consciousness, and introspection as the **method** by which to gain access to consciousness, determined that the strict study of behaviour by the best laboratory methods of experiment, observation and verification, would prove the key to **understanding** humankind as just another (however special) natural creature.

The leading figure in this revolution was J. B. Watson and in 1913, in a famous paper, he proposed the severely scientistic account of the study of behaviour as a result of environmental conditioning and the strategies of adaptation learned by species in the course of evolution (he was much influenced, naturally, by Darwin's great book, *The Origin of Species*, 1851). In Watson's view, the human being is born blank, and develops personality and **intelligence** through its **experience** of life. Attributes are not inherited but learned. Behavioural psychology – a science of behaviour to be amassed by observation, hypothesis-testing and the accumulation of data – will also provide means of correcting and controlling human behaviour for the better (for a while his views had considerable influence in penology and prison policy). These ideas struck strong chords at the time, and left still-active traces in the practice of psychology, not least because of their implicit view of the original **equality** of human beings, who all start out as blank receptors and only gain **power** and status according to their life chances.

Watson's work was promulgated and given worldwide publicity by his follower B. F. Skinner, whose theories of conditional **learning** controlled by carefully graded systems of punishment and reward gave rise to the fears of totalitarian planning for the production of perfectly socialised but radically unfree human creatures satirised in Aldous Huxley's novel, *Brave New World* (1930). Skinner sailed through all objections, insisting that psychology cannot gain access to mental events and can only remain a science by studying what is visible, which is to say, behaviour, and that only by disciplined and **objective** study of behaviour can anything be inferred about so-called inner states.

Skinner's case was badly damaged by Noam Chomsky who, in a classic book-length essay, pointed out that **language** cannot be understood behaviourally, since all human beings may invent hitherto unheard and entirely unprecedented sentences which they could not have learned from their conditioning. Nonetheless, behaviourism still thrives as an active part of the discipline of psychology, and remains malignantly influential and successful in marketing and consumer research.

FURTHER READING

Noam Chomsky (1971), *Problems of Knowledge and Freedom*. Harmondsworth: Penguin.
H. J. Eysenck (1959), *The Uses and Abuses of Psychology*. Harmondsworth: Penguin.
Louise Porter (2007), *Behaviour in Schools*. Maidenhead: Open University Press.
B. F. Skinner (1967), *Beyond Freedom and Dignity*. Harmondsworth: Penguin.
E. L. Thorndike (1911), *Animal Intelligence*. New York: Macmillan.

behaviour

Boredom

Given how frequently this **concept** is invoked to explain **behaviour** on either side of the contested classroom, it is surprising how little thought it has been given. John Berger suggests that it be understood as 'an awareness of the slow death of one's faculties', but this seems a bit protracted for **school** life. Medieval moralists named 'accedia' a mortal sin, and by this seemed to mean a despairing failure to find God's meaning in life. French symbolist poets of the late nineteenth century led by Baudelaire wrote of the *ennui* they suffered, which transpired in their poems as a kind of attitudinal listlessness towards the sameness of life's events, the dreary predictability of their emotions, and above all towards the moronic respectability and dull conventionality of bourgeois life.

This gets closer to contemporary usage, the more so since the *avant-gardistes* of the artistic world in Paris and London pioneered the use of the mind-altering drugs, particularly opium, by then being heavily (and legally) imported from China. These drugs, along with brandy and absinthe, were seized on eagerly as antidote to the repetitious emptiness and boredom of ordinary life.

Such a use of course anticipates by a century and more the present-day recourse to successor refinements as cocaine and heroin, the deadly consumer **choices** on the way to stimulated pleasure-dromes. But the boredom of which the 14-year-old pupil complains seems to be prompted by the not unappealing expectation that life should always be (instantly) absorbing.

One reply to this demand is that life simply cannot be. Large segments of it – queuing, listening, travelling, waiting, polite necessity, unnecessary accident – just *are* boring, and no one can help it. So too are the necessities of **learning**, whether by heart or practice. The poor teacher does his or her best to enliven as much learning as he or she can, but it's an impossible task.

At the same time, one may speculate that the demands for immediate **interest** and the wailing response, 'it's boring, miss' may have their roots in some soil of the present **culture** which feeds a kind of arrogant refusal to be forced to *any* pedagogic task and which fills the veins of those who reject out of hand the world of scholarly or technical learning as boring, replacing it with a preference for mind-numbing forms of time-killing: heavy metal music, contentless mobile phone conversations, death-ray computer games.

That this kind of diagnosis is always ready on the lips of middle-aged teachers doesn't mean it's wrong. But it isn't much help, although it is terribly boring to the teacher always to be warding off charges of boringness. Perhaps the best (or only) device is to try to force self-reflection on the student, to indicate that boredom must at times be accommodated, carefully to show what is deeply interesting in what has been dismissed as boring, and by the same token, discreetly to analyse the boring superficiality and utter tedium of so much of the consumer culture brandished by pupils as badges of interestingness.

Lastly, it might be added that there are different forms of boredom, and that the kind of gentle boredom accompanying a condition of mild dreaminess – looking vaguely at a nice view, waiting at a level crossing, staring at a bowl of flowers, playing idly with the cat – may prove to be as necessary and restorative a soul-medicine as any amount of high, old intellectual or other life.

boredom

Bureaucracy

This is a word and a **concept** rarely used with any other than a downward inflexion. The yellow press is forever blaming difficulties in hospitals on the money supposedly squandered on the bureaucracy instead of being spent on honest nurses and hardworking young doctors. Yet it is plain that all the matters of life and death, along with those of the ordinary administration of clean sheets, accurate doses of medicine, punctual delivery of meals on wheels, all the extraordinarily detailed and ceaseless business of a hospital turn on an efficient bureaucracy. The same is just as true of **schools**, police work, fire services, universities, benefits' offices, highways' agencies, rail and air traffic controls, and on and on, all the buzzing, unstoppable activity of what we call public services even when they are privatised. Our daily world is the product of bureaucratic labour; in a mass **society**, mechanised, computerised, mobile, always at **work**, ever more numerous, it cannot be otherwise, and honouring the bureaucrats as well as watching them carefully is surely a mark of maturity.

Perhaps the very term makes people jumpy because the suffix '-cracy' on any prefix indicates **authority** and rule, and some people resent the idea of being ruled by keepers of the files. For there are good and bad ways to run a bureaucracy, and both have become more emphatic and unignorable as heavier duties have been piled onto the administrative officials of the society. (It should be added that all this is true of the necessary bureaucracies of commercial corporations as well, but its officers don't exactly rule over the rest of us.)

The great German sociologist, Max Weber, was the first to grasp how momentous was the change brought to society by the coming of the bureaucracy and across his comparatively short but productive **career** (he died at 56 in 1920) he codified what it was and is that we expect from a good bureaucracy. He did so, however, on a doleful note; modern life, Weber concluded, was locked in an 'iron cage' of 'rationalisation' (the word is his invention) which doused the enchantment of **experience** and reduced everything to means-end planning.

The bureaucrats, he thought, were not responsible for this 'disenchantment', but their **methods** confirmed it. The bureaucrat takes authority from the legal nouns which confer it. He or she is strictly bound by legal rules and administers their authority (hence what looks, from the other side of the counter, like bureaucratic inflexibility). To that extent, the bureaucrat is not a person but an *official* representing an *im*personal order. He or she is assigned to a specific sphere of **competence**, and may not transgress its boundaries. Each official is placed in a hierarchy, and difficulties are resolved not by discretion but by 'reference upwards'. Officials cannot participate in the ownership of the bureaucracy, nor can they benefit financially (beyond their fixed wages) from the discharge of their duties.

These well-known conditions issue in three expectations on the part of the public. Our first expectation is that bureaucrats have **competence** in their sphere; they keep the files perfectly. This is competence in its dual sense: the first, of the official's adequacy to the office, the second, of his or her **powers** to effect what is required of the office, to turn efficiency into efficacy. The second of our expectations is that bureaucratic *procedures* shall be proper and intelligible, as well as making available avenues of redress when things go wrong. Thirdly, our expectation is that the affairs we each of us submit to the official for administration shall be dealt with anonymously, and that this **principle** adheres to both sides of the counter. All the personal peculiarities of both client and official are irrelevant; if this principle of anonymity is violated, trouble follows. (This is easily seen on those occasions in countries where bribery is endemic; because bribes are personal, they must remain invisible.)

All these strange but familiar social conventions and exchanges generate the abstract and exotic **language** of bureaucratic **management** which leaks out into domestic life. Peter Berger points out the presence of the memorandum notebook or whiteboard kept near the telephone or in the kitchen in many middle-**class** houses, and the principle of orderly planning by diary, the tyranny of the filing cabinet and the storing of documents have all been extended, for better and worse, deep into **individual** routines by the omnipresence of the house computer.

The presence of bureaucracy in schools is and must be everywhere, and every teacher must be an efficient bureaucrat, handling files and dealing with administrative matters with entire competence. At the same time, however, he or she is not exactly an 'official', nor is a pupil a 'client'. The bureaucratic necessities of school need to be softened and humanised accordingly.

FURTHER READING

Hannah Arendt (1968), *Eichmann in Jerusalem*. New York: Viking.

Peter L. Berger and Brigitte Berger (1973), *The Homeless Mind: Modernisation and Consciousness*. Harmondsworth: Penguin.

Max Weber (1964), *The Theory of Social and Economic Organisation*. New York: Free Press.

key concepts in
education

To show all students how to aim at a career became a prime and proud function of **schools** throughout the wealthy parts of the Western world after the end of World War II. Until 1939, in a country with very different systems of production, British schools largely expected to disperse their pupils to local industries and services according to the customs and expectations of neighbourhood and social **class** at a time when those were more settled and taken-for-granted than they are nowadays. **Equality** of opportunity wasn't at that time such a powerful political value, and as the subsequently notorious Norwood Report of 1939 put it, it just so happened that there were three types of pupil – the academic, the technical and the practical (meaning manual labourers) – and these were suitably matched by being sent to the three kinds of school which cultivated their talents: grammar, technical and elementary (later secondary modern).

The Second World War, however, brought about a huge shift in social expectations, especially in the industrial working class. If its members were expected to fight and, plentifully, die for the sake of national liberty, then it wanted its children to have a much better chance of prosperity and social advance than was there when war broke out.

Hence the career structures of class-bound old Britain were loosened up a little, for at least the period 1945–79. Universities were expanded and new ones created, heavy, old industries (coal, steel, shipbuilding, cars) were either automated or declined, the mass migration of ambitious young men and women from north to south-east began, and careers advisers were appointed in every school, expected to counsel students on suitable jobs and to build connections with sympathetic industries and services. To find satisfying careers became the justifiable goal of most of those leaving school, and schools themselves were informally judged on their success in the task of finding them. One key **value** of the school was that it would do its best to ensure the commemoration of the parent generation in the more prosperous lives of their children.

Thereafter, the ideal course of a career would move, at proper intervals, from **training** and apprenticeship to qualification to assorted promotions to seniority and was completed in the happiest cases by arrival at the top, either as boss of one's own show or amongst the **elite** and powerful. This narrative held tightest for the professions but it was written into all such male trades as railwayman, policeman, steelworker, coalminer, carworker, civil service clerk, tax official and so forth. Until the social earthquakes of the 1960s, girls were more rarely designated careers but found employment only before marriage and childbirth.

A career, therefore, became established as a formative, universally intelligible narrative in the value-realm of **work**, and is just as powerful today. The **idea** is, however, in crisis. As manufacturing industry has moved to the Far East and as information and **communication** technology has made all but senior **management** into computer operators in service industries, the **competences** demanded of a career are quickly learned. Meanwhile, at the same time, innovations in ICT and systems of short-run production make for frequent career breaks, and regular periods of unemployment, punitive work regimes and, as a consequence, loss of worker continuity and solidarity, have broken up the old story of a career except for the wealthy elite.

Even in the professions (including teaching) these same tendencies have disrupted continuity of membership, reduced artistry to **technique** and destroyed institutional memory. The crisis is unmistakable and acute. It requires a radical diminution of the productivity routines exemplified by Walmart and the big supermarkets, and concerted efforts (of the sort pioneered at Xerox and in the NHS) to throw away rule books and assembly-line methods, and return trust and **responsibility** to the **skills** and **intelligence** of the workforce.

FURTHER READING

John Seely Brown and Paul Duguid (2007), *The Social Life of Information*. Cambridge, MA: Harvard Business School.

Simon Head (2005), *The New Ruthless Economy: Work and Power in the Digital Age*. Oxford: Oxford University Press.

Richard Sennett (2007), *The Culture of the New Capitalism*. New Haven: Yale University Press.

Childhood

Childhood is a far from fixed category, although it was probably the wide circulation of the Christian gospels after the fifth century CE or so which first gave the **concept** moral and religious force. Nonetheless, as Philippe Ariès, historian of childhood, points out, in almost all paintings up to the middle of the eighteenth century children appear as miniature adults, wearing cut-down versions of their parents' clothes, mostly playing (as in Brueghel's famous painting *Children's Games*) with their parents' utensils or with a tiny number of ritual toys (tops and whips, rag dolls, skipping ropes).

Certainly until the mid-nineteenth century, children were pressed into **work**, especially in poor families, by the time they were five or six, and were until some years older regarded as decidedly provisional members of the family because of the high rates of child mortality (in 1690, it has been estimated, 45 per cent of the population would have been children, but life expectation at birth was only 32, and 0–10 the most lethal years). Marriage (for Romeo and Juliet) took place at 15 or so, and innumerable children in the seventeenth century were not only in work, they were orphans, their most important membership being not so much the family as the whole working household where they laboured, ate and were sheltered.

It is only about the middle of the eighteenth century that something like a modern conception of childhood begins to emerge with what the historian of families, Lawrence Stone, believes was a new growth in the sentiments of conjugal love and family affection. Certainly, portraits of children in wealthy families of that time suggest not only the design of a new kind of wardrobe for children but also the advent of many toys and of a new area for play, the nursery.

In the following decades, poets such as Wordsworth and Blake made childhood into a special and sacred category with its peculiar **wisdom** and its treasured innocence. By the time Dickens was writing of children in the 1840s and after, his wonderful campaigning prose had chimed with strong national feeling that children needed protection from the horrific conditions in which they were forced to labour. Factory inspectors were appointed after 1842 to ensure a limitation in the number of hours worked and at least a minimum of care, and as Britain moved towards a system of compulsory national **education** (formalised by Parliament in 1870) children were transformed into pupils and a special building, the **school**, designated for their occupation from age five or six until eleven.

This short history reads like a **progress**, and in some ways that is correct. Over the same period, the law came to recognise the child as a special kind of legal condition, and children were gradually assigned legal **rights** of a different sort from those of adults. These changes took a long time. It was only in 1985 that all flogging in school was abolished by law.

Nonetheless, childhood remains a much disputed territory. Advocates of **freedom** in education protest on behalf of a much less tightly schooled childhood, while governments seek, with the best intentions, more and more to drill and measure the life of classrooms. At the same time, the systems of capitalist production seek to extend their profits in a large, underexploited section of the population on which parents now confer large amounts of spending **power**. This in turn loosens the hold of the school. It is much to be feared that childhood remains a site of struggle between the social forces which make for free and fulfilled citizens, and those determined to bend unformed **individuals** to darker purposes. In these circumstances, it now seems as if childhood itself has once more been lost, and many children (as teachers daily see) become as a result little boiling vats of angry egotism and sexual precocity.

FURTHER READING

Phillipe Ariès (1973), *Centuries of Childhood*. Harmondsworth: Penguin.
Peter Coveney (1967), *The Image of Childhood*. Harmondsworth: Penguin.
Melanie Klein (1975), *The Psychoanalysis of Children*. London: Hogarth Press.
Lawrence Stone (1977), *The Family, Sex and Marriage 1500–1800*. London: Weidenfeld and Nicolson.

Choice

Choice is one of the most invoked **values** of **liberal** and consumer **society**, and also one of the most distorted and misunderstood. It is, after all, a central premise of liberalism that individuals shall have the **freedom** to become whatever they choose to become. The act of choice is by this token the vindicating moment of the doctrine. To choose is to be autonomous and inasmuch as choosing a government is the defining procedure of **democracy** (tyrants or incompetents can be dismissed in an election), the vote is the emblem of political choice. The doctrine of **rights** further corroborates the importance of choice, since to insist on one's rights is to endorse oneself as an individual who is not to be violated by others or by the government, but who chooses to declare him- or herself as living in a free state. Rights permit choices, and the marketplace is only the most obvious arrangement for the exercise of choice.

'The market' has expanded to become a metaphor for a free society. The European Union, for instance, began life as a 'Free Trade Area' and then became the 'Common Market'. Now it is a 'Union', it finds itself torn by factions for whom the political idea of union is at odds with the ideals of free trade and open marketing, precisely because a polity (in the now old-fashioned word) is not a market, and requires of its members that they act not as competitors but as citizens commonly preoccupied with commitments to a shared good and common goals.

The whole habitual **structure** of public life is, however, adjusted to the ideal of choice as the core operation of selfhood and the proof of freedom. Government policy in all the leading economies and the richest countries is managed in terms of what choices voters may be expected or persuaded to make. Pollsters, focus groups and market researchers are employed to test samples of the population for the 'ordinality' (that is, the ordering of preferences and the ascription of relative importance to choices) so that government becomes the fine tuning of consumer choice: choice of hospitals and doctors, choice of **schools** and universities, let alone of individual teachers. A level and degree choices become **subject** to marketing techniques, and subjects such as classics or chemistry chosen in insufficient numbers are dumped in the dustbin of history, however important they may be to cultural memory or physical necessity.

Conventional politics and the forms of cultural life set impassable limits to the activity of choice. We cannot choose what is not there to be chosen; choices can only be made for the alternatives on offer, and it is a fierce test of the **imagination** to see beyond what is on offer, and to argue for possibilities outside the sort of boxes one is invited to tick.

So the limitations of the value of choice are both strongly protected and hard to see. The usual notion is that choice is best pictured in the insouciant freedom of the supermarket, where the happy consumer has to choose between brands of orange juice or bottled water, toothpastes or tights. In point of fact, as the more refined studies of consumer **behaviour** teach us, consumer choice is as much constrained by habit and familiarity as by price or novelty. We choose what we're used to, we avoid pointless risks, we like the occasional change (of governments or beers) for no other reason than that 'It's time for a (bit of a) change'.

There isn't much here to justify choice as quite so high a value as **liberalism** makes it. Moreover, choosing is not always the right verb to apply to our coming to a decision. The leading French philosopher of the 1940s and 1950s, Jean-Paul Sartre, also put choice at the centre of his doctrine of existentialism. He saw momentous life choices as being the very peaks of our **identity**, and cowardly refusals to make them as acts of 'bad faith'. But the kind of choices he had in mind were not those of the market researcher's list of alternative boxes to tick. Sartre's kind of choice was between joining or not joining the French Resistance to fascism, or setting off to become a Marxist anti-bourgeois revolutionary. It has been objected that these are not decisions to be accurately described as choices. Rather, they result from perhaps painful self-scrutiny in which the individual reviews his or her life allegiances and contemplates the crisis of the moment until able to conclude what *must be done*. At such a moment one does not so much choose as wait for the path towards action to become clear, and then follow it.

However, choice as defined in contemporary politics, marketing and schools is with us for the duration, and it is worth knowing that so-called 'rational choice theory' is an active branch of economics offering to tell us how our choosing mechanisms work. According to its rule book, each of us seeks to 'maximise our utilities', and rationality is defined as performing those actions most likely to bring about our desires. This cuts out any discussion of shared purposes towards common goods. The critic of rational choice **theory**, Jon Elster, has however pointed out that there are times when the best way to decide what to do is to toss a coin, and others when the best thing to do is to *minimise* desires and utilities. Elster is much concerned to multiply motivations and complicate the concept of choice. Rational self-interest is constantly overborne by the weight of social bonds and customs. Motivations are too readily explained by consequences. It seems to be the case that choice may be a more manifold business than at first sight, and in any case less important than is generally supposed.

Choice in **education**, much vaunted by the government, often turns out to be an illusion. Parents may choose, but do not get their choice. Middle-class parents, especially in cities, may choose a school further afield, so children become disconnected from their **community**. In a rural context, there is only one school to choose anyway.

FURTHER READING

Stephen J. Ball (2008), *The Education Debate*. London: Policy Press.
Alan Donagan (1987), *Choice: The Essential Element in Human Action*. London: Macmillan.
Jon Elster (ed.) (1986), *Rational Choice*. Oxford: Blackwell.
B. Fischhoff and P. Slovic (1980), *Cognitive Processes in Choice and Decision Behaviour*. Hillsdale, NY: Erlbaum.

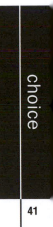
choice

As an educational and political **concept**, citizenship has one of the longest pedigrees in this book. It may be traced, in very early formulations, to Plato's discussions of the duties of (male) members of the Republic, and more specifically, in Aristotle's lectures developing Plato (the *Nicomachean Ethics* and the *Politics*), where he describes the ideal functioning of the *polis*, which is to say the 'polity' or institution of self-government. There citizens will debate and settle the common good of the **society** according to common **principles** of rational discourse.

The **idea** was given formal and legal definition first as the Roman Empire bestowed citizenship on its auxiliary troops, and then in the passionate and bloodstained arguments in classical Rome as such eloquent opponents of tyranny as Cicero and Seneca opposed in the Forum and in the courts of law the long slide of their republic into subordination to the Emperors. Their arguments were then resumed, almost a thousand years later, by theorists of the city-states of northern Italy as they too struggled to come at legal embodiments of order and liberty, and the demands made upon their citizens that they look after these cherished **values** for themselves.

These Italian cities – Lucca, Florence, Pisa, Siena, and countless others – re-inaugurated a debate picked up in the several crises of Europe and North America between 1500 and 1900 as different geographies gathered themselves into nations. In England, the debate between Parliament and King about civic **freedom** and royal **authority** erupted in 1642 into a civil war which resolved the matter by providing 'the freeborn Englishman' (in the great phrase of the day) with a constitutional monarch. In France in 1789, the revolutionary victors even insisted that every French person renounce outdated social titles and be addressed simply as 'citizen', a badge of proud nationality as well as of rights to liberty, **equality** and fraternity. At the same time, after the 1776 war of independence, Americans wrote their mighty constitution in order to legislate for ever the **rights**, freedoms and corresponding duties of the citizen.

As the world shook itself into a pattern of nation-states, each new or reconstituted nation prescribed a charter for its citizens, whether in the new Germany and Italy of the 1870s, post-revolutionary Russia in 1921 or the peoples of the former imperial colonies, from India in 1947 onwards.

Since these **developments** accompanied a programme of industrialisation and its essential instrument, a national system of compulsory **education**, it was during those uneven but drastic transformations that schoolchildren were instructed in the local principles of citizenship.

Since Britain was in the vanguard of imperial **powers** divesting themselves of their colonies, she too tabulated new rules for her own **subjects**. A British academic, T. H. Marshall, published *Citizenship and Social Class* in 1946, which set out the rights of the citizen in that novelty, the welfare state. These were rights to freedoms of speech and property, freedom (for all adults) to take part in the political process without restrictions as to wealth or status and, above all, freedom of personal being and movement assured by a minimum share in the collective wealth of society and the guarantee of adequate safety from time and chance as upheld by national entitlements to benefits and health care. Although education was central to the transmission of these rights after 1949, it is obvious that a definition of citizenship grounded only in rights is insufficient to teach those duties citizens must meet in order to preserve their freedom.

Recognising a widespread softening in the social bonds which hold society together, national governments since 1990 have inserted an obligation into the National **Curriculum** to teach by unspecified means such civic attributes as self-**discipline**, a spirit of enterprise, a sense of social **responsibility** and so forth. It is to be feared, however, that without a Bill of Rights enshrining civic principles in law, the image of the common good, towards which a citizen strives by definition, has little chance of discovering its reality.

Citizenship is now a National Curriculum subject which is taught, tested and inspected alongside others. One **objective** is to develop pupils into 'informed citizens', who will play a full part in society. Themes which are covered include human rights, equality and diversity, crime, local democracy, and global issues. Some **schools** teach it as a discrete subject on the timetable, and some have integrated units of **work** where relevant into other subjects, such as history, geography or religious education. For example, the unit on 'the significance of the media in society' fits well into an English scheme of work.

FURTHER READING

T. H. Marshall (1946), *Essays on the Welfare State*. London: Allen and Unwin.
Simon Schama (1989), *Citizens*. New York: Knopf.

Class is in the first instance a neutral term indicating a boundary set around a selection or population of similar entities. In a school, a 'class' is a specific group of pupils – who may not appear to be 'similar entities' at all. Classifying the world is a fundamental human necessity by way of making it intelligible. Once things that are alike are put together, they can imaginably be brought under human control. During the disputes among the great figures who brought modern science into being at the turn of the sixteenth century, Francis Bacon wrote 'count and classify', and the ordering of classification by numbers is the foundation of science.

Schemes of classification are now known by a term borrowed from biology as taxonomies and fixing the membership and size of classes ('set theory') is a field of creative innovation in contemporary mathematics and its application to the dominant fields of bio-engineering and particle physics. The population of a class or set is wholly determined by the **identity** of its members, but there are two monster difficulties for the scientists: first, there are empirically unobservable particles whose existence they deduce but cannot measure; second, all set or class theory hovers on the point of contradiction. Bertrand Russell pointed out in his celebrated paradox that if a set or class is determined by a common property, then the set of all normal sets, that is those which are not their own sole member, is, if a member of itself, unattachable to a set. If it is not a member of itself, it must (but cannot) belong to the set of all normal sets. This century-old puzzle is more than a mathematical game; it makes practical (and therefore understanding) classifying highly unstable.

However, the everyday meaning of class is almost wholly sociological and political. Class then means social class, and social classification has long been fixed for reference purposes (and also much modified) by the sometime *Registrar-General's Classification of Occupations*. This HMSO publication assigned a descending ladder of occupations: class A (**professional** and managerial), B (technical and supervisory), C (divided into C1 and C2 according to qualifications and status) (clerical and skilled manual), D (unskilled manual) and E, which was a ragbag into which the unemployed and unclassifiable were dumped.

This summary classification has been softened to accommodate both social sensitivities and the slipperiness of many of the categories: how technical is clerical? how qualified is this computer operator? Social class in sociological inquiry has also been much exercised by the apparently increased porousness of class categories, particularly in the extraordinary efflorescence of forms of new occupation generated by the revolution in electronic technology together with the headlong energy of turbo-capitalism since the 1980s. The necessity for all employees to shift their jobs at frequent intervals and retrain for a new one, as well as the small but noticeable minority of people resigning from social competition and trying to shape a livelihood by the statutes of modest self-sufficiency, all make for class indistinction.

These changes mean that the old certainties of class as a dependable **structure** with a regular membership and a hierarchy of rewards have departed for good. One way of refining and giving density to the discussion of class has for half a century and more been to go beyond the structures of pay and occupation to the **culture** of social classes, their **art** and entertainment, their **language**, accent and manners, their moral **values** and political affiliation. It is by these small public dramas that most people nowadays make their necessary class **judgements** and adjustments, and sociologists (and teachers) speak far less than they used to of social class now that its signs and meanings slip and slide about all the time.

Nonetheless, there can be no doubt that in **education** above all social activity the signs of class are highly visible and the force of social structure as violent and unstoppable as ever. One unhappy but vivid phrase emerged from the new class uncertainties of the 1980s, and that was 'the underclass'. These were the ill-educated, the helpless, the migrants, the unemployable (frequently because of the disappearance of the industry which trained them), the sick, the old; they were the poor.

The poor today make for a highly visible, largely unseen social class, a substantial proportion of the **society** left behind by the amazing growth in national wealth these past 20 years. It is a strange corollary that the neglect in political terms of the making of a new super-rich class, some one or two per cent of society sailing out of reach of taxation to paradise islands in the South Seas, is part of that same curious blindness to the corrigible condition of poverty which is caused by our losing our grip on class **theory**.

Social class is not difficult to think about for all its changeability. Every teacher needs a rough-and-ready theory of class in the classroom, and needs it in order to follow the ideals of **equality, justice,** fulfilment, happiness, which are the point of the **vocation** of **teaching**. Nevertheless, despite all a teacher's efforts, family income is still the best indicator of educational attainment.

FURTHER READING

Stephen J. Ball (2008), *The Education Debate.* London: Policy Press.
Basil Bernstein (1971–75), *Class, Codes and Control,* vols 1–3. London: Routledge and Kegan Paul.
J. W. B. Douglas (1964), *The Home and the School.* London: MacGibbon and Kee.
Patrick Joyce (ed.) (1995), *Class.* Oxford: Oxford University Press.

key concepts in education

Communication

The word 'communication' comes from the Latin *communis*, a fellowship, so it is related to the noun 'community', and the adjective 'common' which signifies features that are shared with others. 'Communication' is the process by which **individuals** and organisations share information with others.

The most obvious form of communication is **language**, although looks, glances, gestures and expressions (body language) convey a great deal. In the development of language, the first words to emerge were probably very practical ones – fire, forest, wolf and so on. More abstract terms would come later: love, happiness, loyalty. This is where the problems in communication started, as abstract words never mean exactly the same to different people. Individuals modify their understanding of words according to their own **experiences**. Even an apparently simple word such as 'bird' signifies a wide range of images: to me it might suggest a homely sparrow; to someone else, a particularly vicious seagull. Such discontinuities of interpretation can lead to misunderstanding between individuals. Some of the words in this book (for example, '**progress**' or '**spiritual**') have very different meanings for different people, which can lead to impassioned argument and debate. No two people will read a poem in exactly the same way; this is why literary **criticism** is such a huge industry. Writers exploit these ambiguities in their **work**.

Social construction theory assumes that normal development involves individuals acquiring the language and associated cognitive **skills** needed to learn to communicate, and through this to construct new **knowledge** and skills. There is also an assumption that 'communication skills' can be developed by effective teaching. Unfortunately for some individuals, particularly those on the autistic spectrum, their ability to use language in this way to gain insight into the minds (and hence social worlds) of others is often impaired. The extent of this impairment can vary enormously, but for classically autistic individuals, teachers cannot assume that they can communicate in the same way as their peers who are able to develop an **understanding** of the working of others' minds.

A 'medium' is a means of communication; hence the use of the word for a person who is supposed to receive messages from the spirit world.

The term 'mass media' signifies all the types of communication that are out in the public domain, such as newspapers, television and radio. Electronic media are the newest form of communication.

The term 'information and communication technology' (ICT) shows the dual purpose of the worldwide web. It provides access to data and factual information, although even these, depending on how they are presented, can be biased and subjective. It was soon realised that there was no need to restrict electronic media to sharing factual information, and now ICT provides more intuitive and interactive forms of written communication than traditional types of writing, while still stimulating the use of internal language (thinking). It is the interactive nature of many websites that enables individuals to communicate with a far wider range of people than would previously have been the case. This is exciting; it also has its dangers.

ICT is transforming the range of teaching styles, not only through interactive whiteboards, which can be used in a traditional classroom, but also through the development of 'virtual learning environments' which enable pupils to work on their own at their own pace. **Techniques** such as these were pioneered by the Open University with their 'computer-assisted learning' and broadcast lectures, but the level of sophistication, and interaction, is now infinitely greater.

FURTHER READING

David Buckingham (2007), *Beyond Technology: Children's Learning in the Age of Digital Culture*. Cambridge: Polity Press.

Manuel Castells (1996), *The Rise of the Network Society*. Oxford: Blackwell.

Bryn Holmes and John Gardner (2006), *E-learning: Concepts and Practice*. London: Sage.

David Holmes (2005), *Communication Theory: Media, Technology and Society*. London: Sage.

Fred Inglis (1990), *Media Theory*. Oxford: Blackwell.

Marshall McLuhan (2001), *Understanding Media*. Abingdon: Routledge.

Raymond Williams (1966), *Communications*. Harmondsworth: Penguin.

Community is a word almost impossible to utter with hostility. It is also, like so many of our **concepts**, so generally applied to such differing conditions that it is difficult to see how it can carry such a heavy weight of **value**. Thus, newspapers regularly speak of the community of nations, large disparate groups scattered through the **society** are associated in terms of belief, employment or geography as communities ('the Muslim community', 'the fishing community', 'the village community'), although in every case one can detect an appeal to a higher and well-acknowledged value.

This is the value given to direct, close and immediate social relations. The word itself expresses the commonness of the **qualities** implied, and community is counterposed to society as meaning those direct, mutual, interdependent relations people hope to share with their neighbours, in their work places, in their home township, wherever faces are recognisable, touch is physical, cooperation is expressible in visible action. Communities are, according to these meanings, held together by the tangible familiarities of custom, **tradition**, solidarity, as opposed to the abstract legalities of contract, law and the routines of compulsory practice which define one's relationship with society.

Implicit in its contemporary use is a wistfulness for something people believe, with **justice**, has been lost in modern life. This is the natural, self-explanatory rhythm of community in an agrarian, local and orderly past, bound by common necessity to known and loved places, tasks and festivals, united in common beliefs and by the reassurance of membership. The French sociologist Emile Durkheim made the distinction between societies fastened together in implicit solidarity and undivided labour which he called 'mechanistic', and societies whose intricate systems of divisions of specialised labour meant that they were held together not by tasks performed in common but in specialised separation and explicit obligation; such societies he called 'organicist' and they are the modern ones.

The frequent appeal to community often suggests a longing for the older kind of society, overlooking the fact that membership requires exclusion by definition, and that all exclusive communities are chronically liable to victimisation, suppressed abuse, bigotry and a suspicious hostility towards any strangers. By the same token, the looseness and

community

49

provisionality of social bonding which has become so usual in late modern societies no doubt makes for weaker communities, but does much for individual **freedom**, open-mindedness and social mobility.

There can, however, be no doubt that the political economies of the twenty-first century break up established communities, turn lifelong **careers** into a series of disjoined and casual jobs, render personal relationships more temporary and detachable, and make it damnably hard to tell oneself an intelligible and continuous life history. Community is then the name for the world we have lost, **education** the **knowledge** industry put to the task of inventing such life history, and **schools** the places where the ideal of community may be kept alive.

In the 1960s, as **comprehensive** education became a national requirement in the hope that it would dissolve some of the bitter enmities of **class**, some new schools were designated 'community colleges', their task and realisation being to re-create communal life by calling to their premises all those of any age who could attend the college at any time of day for the purposes of learning with others, of self-improvement as a common and excellent task.

The idea was to diminish the remoteness of the state schools and to substitute the warmth and nearness of community college ('college' itself having happier associations than 'school'). The story encapsulates the force of the concept of community, with its messages of safety, rootedness, **understanding**. The big issue is belonging, and if a child or a citizen cannot belong to a school, he or she will belong nowhere.

FURTHER READING

Zygmunt Bauman (2001), *Community*. Cambridge: Polity Press.

Emile Durkheim (1915), *Suicide*. London: Allen and Unwin.

Richard Sennett (1996), *The Uses of Disorder: Personal Identity and City Life*. London: Faber.

Competence

For a word which comes into the conversation with such an assured air, 'competence' has unnervingly varied meanings. It begins by being close to 'compete' in the late sixteenth century, and indicated then rivalry in dignity or relative social position. Proceeding with shreds of this meaning on its way, it advanced to take in a man's (in the eighteenth and nineteenth centuries, invariably a man's) sufficiency of income, estate and (though the phrase doesn't arrive until the twentieth century) '**standard** of living'. In this sense, a competence placed a man in more or less comfortable circumstances, he was himself a 'competencer'.

Through the eighteenth century, however, a new sense began to dominate over the old, which nonetheless maintains its presence today, if a bit archaically. The new sense chose, in what was then the novel conditions of civil law courts, and designated legal capacity in a **professional** lawyer, a meaning which quickly became enlarged to become close to modern usage.

To be thoroughly competent, in a job or a role (teacher, parent) is to command respect. A competent bureaucrat wins our trust; he or she carries off **authority** and **responsibility** in the right ways, ways which ensure order, stability and **justice** in handling affairs. Competence therefore embodies a singular **value** in spite of the faint whiff of boringness which attaches to it: one would rather be an inspiring teacher than a competent one, but one might certainly be a popular teacher *and* an *in*competent one.

The term takes on more specialised meaning in linguistic **theory** and therefore in **pedagogy**, where it is contrasted with 'capability'. All human beings are born with an innate **language** capability, but their language competence is what each acquires from social **learning**. Competence refers to an individual's knowledge of his or her language, to the so-called 'surface' rules each masters in order to be able to create and understand an infinite number of new and intelligible sentences. Competence is then further distinguished by linguists (first in the 1960s by the linguist, Noam Chomsky) from 'performance', which refers to what one actually says. Performance includes hesitations, repetitions, self-corrections, muddles, incomplete utterances, to which we are all liable but which differ from our competence inasmuch as we know the rules but do not always apply them.

competence

51

FURTHER READING

Zygmund Bauman (1995), *Life in Fragments*. Oxford: Blackwell.
Noam Chomsky (1980), *Rules and Representations*. Oxford: Basil Blackwell.
David Crystal (1985), *Linguistics*. Harmondsworth: Penguin.
Avishai Margalit (1995), *The Decent Society*. Cambridge, MA: Harvard University Press.

key concepts in education

Comprehensive

The word 'comprehensive' comes from 'to comprehend', which means to understand but took on the meaning of a full, overarching **understanding**, as in the title of a book published in 1875: *A Comprehensive Survey of the Philosophy of Plato*. It is this sense of being all-inclusive that is signified in the term 'comprehensive **schools**'.

After the 1944 Education Act, local education **authorities** (LEAs) operated a selective system of grammar schools for those children who passed the '11 plus', and 'secondary moderns' for the rest. This system was full of inequalities and anomalies. For example, some authorities had far more grammar school places than others. More girls than boys passed the 11 plus, but there were not extra places available for them, as many authorities had single-sex grammar schools and, if the schools were mixed, the boy–girl ratio was equal.

Many children who failed the 11 plus were demoralised. Friends were split up. Some LEAs started to change the system early on, for example, in 1955 'the LCC had adopted the educational policy of the so-called comprehensive school, where all, whatever their **standards**, were to be educated together up to the age of 15'. In 1965, the government issued a circular requiring all LEAs to have plans to convert their schools into comprehensive schools. The change took place in most parts of the country during the 1970s, but there are still a few places where grammar schools persist. Sometimes they have 'comprehensives' alongside, but obviously these cannot be comprehensive if the higher-attaining pupils have been creamed off.

Some research suggests that under the grammar system in the 1960s and 1970s, children of higher **ability** did significantly better academically than they do now. This is impossible to prove, as the public **examinations** (which provide measurable data) are completely different from those of 40 years ago. Nevertheless, it is worth noting that in 1968, under the selective system, 18 per cent of pupils left school with five O levels. Today, with a largely comprehensive system, more than 50 per cent leave with five good GCSEs. On the basis of GCSE results, which have been rising steadily, comprehensive schools are very successful.

Areas that still have grammar schools do no better than areas with comprehensive schools. Such a comparison has to be made between authorities where the attainment and socio-economic background of pupils on entry are roughly the same. For example, overall results in 2007 for Kent, which has kept its grammar schools, were not as good as in West Sussex, which is Kent's 'very close' statistical neighbour in terms of socio-economic data, and is organised on fully comprehensive lines.

FURTHER READING

Stephen J. Ball (2008), *The Education Debate*. London: Policy Press.
Caroline Benn (1996), *Thirty years On: Is Comprehensive Education Alive and Well?* Bristol: David Fulton.

key concepts in education

Concept

A concept is an organising **idea** which serves to pick out certain features in an object of thought and distinguishes it from other objects. To conceptualise is therefore fundamental to thinking at all, and we all begin its operation in early infancy. Kant famously wrote 'no percepts without concepts' by which he meant quite literally that we cannot see things without an organising idea to tell us what to see. It is said that the first thing a baby learns to see is a face (which, it is added, may be why we can see faces anywhere – in the folds of a curtain or the head of a flower), and smiles in recognition of the fact that it knows what it sees.

This brings us to a second point about concepts, which is that we may possess a concept without having a word for it. New concepts consistently arise in response to new ways of seeing and evaluating **experience**; old terms are sometimes newly applied to supply a word for a concept which has been invented. (**Culture** is an instance of this, first referring only to the cultivation of crops, then as a new concept covering all the expressive forms of a **society** as well as an **education** in those forms, when social commentators found they needed such a term to mount a new kind of argument.)

It is moreover the case that we have words for which there exists *no* corresponding concept. Words of expansive generality such as 'being' or 'infinity' may be used by a particular group of people (theologians, for example) with complete consistency, but it may prove easy enough to show that there is simply no concept answering to their agreed usages. Thus, a group of people may believe that they are in possession of a given concept, and be in fact mistaken. (This is perhaps apparent in those religious sects believing themselves to be chosen for salvation who consequently cut themselves off from the forms of **knowledge**, science in particular, which convincingly suggest that such chosenness is not a concept which means anything.)

There are, therefore, rules and conditions for the use of a concept. It must refer to something determinable in experience. There is usually, but not necessarily, a word corresponding with a concept. The sense of a concept is discoverable by aligning it with related concepts and selecting the most apposite. Thus, in deciding whether to describe an action as 'kind-hearted', we might consider neighbouring terms such as 'loving' or 'generous', and settle for the first because we judge 'loving' to be an exaggeration of the gesture involved and 'generous' inapplicable since no gift was given. In all these cases, however, it is also noteworthy that the rules forbid us to use them disapprovingly: these three terms can only be used to report the action admiringly.

All this is not to say that a concept is always unambiguous or without contradiction. Quite the contrary. Concepts accrue meaning over time, as well as changing from their original usage. They frequently carry forward a residue from past meanings into the present, which may sound a discordant echo. Once powerful religious terms like 'paradise' or 'damnation' still sound that echo even in the most domestic of circumstances. A drastic change in such a word as 'condescension' expresses a strong movement in social manners. In the eighteenth century, superior classes were praised for their 'condescension' in taking notice of their inferiors; in our more egalitarian age, the word connotes an insufferable degree of presumption. Sometimes a word is made to carry two quite different concepts: for instance, literature means the body of classic texts chosen by a society as its best writing; it also means a sheaf of leaflets advertising holidays or new central heating.

Finally, there may be fierce disputes over the meaning of a concept, and indeed when there are, this alerts us to the presence of important shifts in the ascription of social meaning. We have only to think of contention around the question, 'What is **art**?', to be reminded of the urgency of conceptual debate. Confusion and raised voices are intrinsic to the study of all important concepts. That study needs, however, to be practised holistically. There is, in other words, a *wholeness* to the context in which a concept is used. It takes its place in a larger conceptual scheme, as is also plain when we mention art. Art cannot be discussed without reference to that larger conceptual scheme, and the heaven and hell of conceptual dispute are found in fixing the limits of any such scheme.

FURTHER READING

J. L. Austin (1961), 'Are there a priori concepts?' in *Philosophical Papers*. Oxford: Clarendon Press.

Richard Gregory (1971), *The Intelligent Eye*. London: Weidenfeld and Nicolson.

Steven Pinker (2007), *The Stuff of Thought: Language as a Window into Human Nature*. New York: Viking.

Criticism

To be critical is, in everyday conversation, to be a bit anti-social, to be looking for disagreement, to be hard to please. Yet learning how to criticise is the bedrock foundation of **education** and one fundamental activity of thinking. It has, what is more, manifold forms. Far from being merely the habit of picking holes in things and of finding defects in everything, one may be no less critical in creatively imagining circumstances or conditions different from those which prevail, and then pointing out their advantages.

It is usual to counterpose creation to criticism. But when a poet is going through a first draft of a poem improving its rhythms or crossing out one image and substituting another, he or she is criticising *and* creating at the same time. When a physicist looks at his computer screen and sees the symbols dance, he then becomes intent on compelling the symbols into the right order, moving and juggling them until blockage and anomaly are removed, and they issue as a beautiful reflection of the way the particles move. This is a critical-creative activity.

Criticism is not the inviolable sequence of rules to be applied, as logic is. It is shaped by the **principles** of argument of a natural sort, taking in inference (or **judgements** come to not as fixed proofs but as reasonable conclusions, which is what we mostly have to build on), as well as more watertight deductions.

The assertions of argument and our critical responses to them are much richer of meaning than deductive or logical proofs, and this makes not only for uncertainty and confusion but also for the keen pleasures of sorting out what we mean and what we are doing when we criticise. The philosopher J. L. Austin gave the nickname 'performative' to many of our utterances, pointing out that much of the time we are not making propositions – 'this or that is true or false' – but *doing* something else altogether. We might be asserting our authority, propounding a hypothesis, making a joke or trying to deceive. All utterances are 'performative' and part of the business of criticism is to decide what sort of performance is in front of us.

In this latter connection we are all of us nowadays keenly sensitive to the emotive content of argument and its performatives, and part of criticism is to identify what Austin called its 'perlocutionary' or its 'affective' force, that is, how an utterance affects your feelings. This form of criticism directs attention to the idea of speech-*acts* rather than our thinking of everything which is said to us as being a true or false proposition.

These are only two ways of thinking critically, the critical-creative and the analysis of speech-acts. As suggested, criticism may be made coterminous with all the activities of **mind** and its expression in the densely interwoven tapestry of the conversation of a **culture**. The countless **principles** and procedures we have for grasping, rebutting and accepting arguments are the very texture of thought, and irreducible to **theory**. Criticism is rationality in action.

FURTHER READING

Wilfred Carr (1986), *Becoming Critical: Education Knowledge and Action Research*. NSW: Deakin University Press.

F. W. Dauer (1989), *Critical Thinking: An Introduction to Reasoning*. Oxford: Oxford University Press.

I. A. Richards (1929), *Practical Criticism*. London: Chatto and Windus.

John Searle (1969), *Speech Acts*. Cambridge: Cambridge University Press.

Culture is a term for which people often reach if only to describe something hardly more precise than the atmosphere of a neighbourhood or the climate of opinion among a group. At the same time, it is also used to characterise the whole way of life of a people ('the culture of France') or even of the religious beliefs of a sixth of the globe ('the culture of Islam'). As a result, the **concept** of culture, which in these senses is only about 250 years old, comes close to being vacuous. That is to say, it is hard to determine what particular features of the world it is supposed to pick out for attention. It allows so much in, it becomes awash with meanings.

Nonetheless, handled with a bit of care, culture as a concept remains useful and important for identifying those aspects of life which not only accompany everything we do, but shape our doing of it at the same time. Culture, we might say, is the ground of our involuntary being, that upon which we write the figures of our local lives: our politics, our religious observances, our economics, our ethics. It may be analysed and endorsed; it cannot however be planned for.

In its sixteenth-century origins, the word simply connoted human cultivation or tillage of crops. But as we noted in the introduction, a concept may come to be used before there is a single corresponding word which will capture that use. This was the case with culture in the Enlightenment in Germany of the eighteenth century. There, the great poet, Friedrich Schiller, began to commend the whole of artistic endeavour as the surest source of moral wisdom and intelligent emancipation. The **arts**, for Schiller, could provide the fullest possible **education** for an **individual**, conducing to his and her imaginativeness, sensitivity and moral sympathy.

At about the same time, a German philologist, Johann Gottfried Herder, began to speak of the creative **achievements** of a whole people, supremely their **language**, as constituting a single form of life, shaping its members in separate and distinctive ways. Each of these forms of life had its own, singular strengths and characteristics, not necessarily to be assimilated by other forms of life, but valid and precious in and for itself.

These usages launched the dual meaning of culture, a duality not always easy to hold together. In England, the poet, social critic and schools inspector, Matthew Arnold, published in 1868 his *Culture and Anarchy*, in which he defined his key concept as 'the best that has been known and thought'. This book, and the long debate it initiated, confirmed one half of the meaning of the word: its high-minded, idealising and morally earnest meaning.

Only a little time later, however, the new science of anthropology committed its first explorers to the study of the apparent enclosed and self-sufficient ways of life of remote peoples (mostly under British imperial rule). The word 'culture' was then invaluable by way of designating a way or form of life clearly and radically different from the anthropologist's own. Any regular pattern of conduct, belief, custom or ritual became eligible for **inclusion** under its heading, whether child-rearing in Samoa (for Margaret Mead in the 1930s), funerary and burial rites in East Africa (for E. E. Evans-Pritchard in 1944), or cockfights among the Balinese (for Clifford Geertz in the 1950s).

The two meanings – the ideal and the everyday – clearly and sometimes usefully grate in high tension against each other. In a famous book, *Culture and Society* (1958), Raymond Williams wrote the history of the idealising usage of the term. In the same year, Richard Hoggart wrote a pioneering study of the traditional English working class (*The Uses of Literacy*), tabulating its culture in terms of its moral utterances, its jokes and songs, family relationships, food and leisure reading.

The concept retains its dual force. But it has been softened by its broadcast application to such passing phenomena as the success or failure of a **school**, board of directors, a police force or a football team. It retains nonetheless its signal importance as a way of identifying the key **values** and allegiances of different ways of life, and those aspects of them which most matter to their practitioners.

It is a word that schools have to be aware of, as they must ensure that learners make **progress** in their spiritual, moral, social and also cultural development. In practice, the 'cultural' part of this is covered in history (including local history), English (through literature), art, drama and music. Cultural events in school, such as theatre productions or art exhibitions, are celebrated. A multicultural aspect is seen as very important in all parts of the country, not just where the school is working in a context of ethnic diversity. The school must widen pupils' **knowledge** and **experience** of their own and other cultural traditions. It is now very important to say 'other cultures', rather than 'different cultures' – as 'different' implies being different from a **norm**.

FURTHER READING

Matthew Arnold (1990 [1869]), *Culture and Anarchy*, edited by S. Collini. Cambridge: Cambridge University Press.

Seyla Benhabib (2002), *The Claims of Culture*. Princeton: Princeton University Press.

Clifford Geertz (1975), *The Interpretation of Cultures*. London: Hutchinson.

Fred Inglis (2004), *Culture*. Cambridge: Polity Press.

Raymond Williams (1958), *Culture and Society*. Harmondsworth: Penguin.

culture

Curriculum

The word 'curriculum' comes from the Latin *currere*, to run, and so links with 'course' (as for a race). 'Curriculum vitae' is the course of one's life. The word took on the meaning of a course of study. In **schools**, it usually means the full range of **subjects** taught, taken as a whole **experience**. Nowadays, the curriculum is meant to be 'broad and balanced'. It should be enhanced in schools by 'extracurricular' activities, which are the clubs and trips which pupils can choose to join, beyond the basic curriculum.

The essential forms of the academic curriculum in Britain were set by medieval monasteries and then consolidated by the Elizabethan Grammar Schools, there identified as the exclusive subjects of school study. Fundamental to that education was the principle of inwardness in the relation between the knower and the known. Knowledge was intimately bound to the deep structure of the self; this vital connection is now under threat. Of course as compulsory schooling established itself after 1870, social class differences were soon visible in the curriculum, with the old academic subjects allocated to the managerial and propertied classes and what came to be called the 'practical' skills for the working class. Even so, the principle of inwardness – of a personal connection with what one knows and what one does with it – was vehemently taught. Only now is a dislocation of this essential unity becoming apparent, and knowledge is transforming itself into money, divorced from persons and their dedication. Until recently, however varied curricula might have been – and for several decades teachers could pretty well devise their own – there was a shared commitment to knowledge as mattering keenly to those who acquired it.

In 1976, the then prime minister Jim Callaghan made a speech setting out the need for a national curriculum which would provide a common experience for all pupils. One obvious benefit was that children moving schools would be familiar with what was being taught. It was not until 1989 that the 'National Curriculum Orders' came into force for Key Stage 1, and 1990 for Key Stages 2–4.

Since 1990, the National Curriculum has been revised at least three times. This has reduced the content of some subjects, but has also added new areas. The 16 subjects are now: art and design, **citizenship**, design and technology, English, geography, history, information technology, mathematics, modern foreign language, music, physical education, science, religious education, careers education, work-related learning, and personal, social and health education.

This curriculum is compulsory until the end of Key Stage 3 (age 14). What is now called the '14–19 curriculum' has more flexibility, and allows pupils to have more choice. It also introduces vocational subjects. The curriculum at all key stages is still designed to meet the economic needs of society; nowadays, workers are required to be flexible, technologically adept, independent and creative (without going too far – iconoclasts are not encouraged). There is an emphasis on **skills** which can be adapted to a range of contexts.

The latest documentation from the QCA (Qualifications and Curriculum Authority) gives the following aims for the curriculum – that it should 'enable all young people to become successful learners who enjoy **learning**, make **progress** and achieve; confident individuals who are able to live safe, healthy and fulfilling lives; responsible citizens who make a positive contribution to society' (working draft, September–December, 2007). These aims cannot be achieved just within lessons. It is the whole-school experience which will produce successful learners, confident individuals and responsible citizens. This experience includes the atmosphere and environment in school, the way **behaviour** is managed, relationships between staff and pupils, and opportunities for pupils to make decisions, solve problems and collaborate with each other. Aspects such as these used to be called the 'hidden curriculum', and it was recognised that pupils would be influenced by them. Nowadays it is clearly acknowledged that every part of school life affects pupils, and helps to develop their confidence and **responsibility** – or, if badly managed, turns them off altogether. Some schools plan particularly well for elements such as links with their local **community** or with the wider world, charity work, or artistic events. All schools are aware of the importance of school dinners, and do their best to encourage a healthy lifestyle. Some schools become beacons of cultural diversity.

As well as the term 'extracurricular', which covers all activities outside the timetabled, subject-based curriculum, there is also the term 'cross-curricular'. This refers to themes or skills which are developed in different subjects across the curriculum, such as literacy, or the use of ICT. These should not be left to chance, but need to be carefully planned, so that all (for example) opportunities to make individual presentations in different subjects are clearly identified. In the case of

literacy across the curriculum, all teachers need to be prepared to teach the specific reading and writing skills required in their subject.

FURTHER READING

N. Entwhistle (ed.) (1990), 'Designing and evaluating the curriculum', in *Handbook of Educational Ideas and Practices*. London: Routledge.

Thomas W. Hewitt (2006), *Understanding and Shaping the Curriculum: What we Teach and Why*. London: Sage.

A. V. Kelly (2004), *The Curriculum: Theory and Practice*. London: Sage.

D. Lawton and C. Chitty (eds) (1988), *The National Curriculum*. London: Institute of Education.

www.curriculum.qca.org.uk

www.curriculumonline.gov.uk

Democracy

Democracy is the single most dominant and longest-lived political system in history. It started out from the tiny city-state of Athens two and a half thousand years ago and has long since established itself as the set of ideal **principles** for the ordering of the just **society**. Its world **authority** is now greater than that of any one religion, and its moral status such that even the worst despot tries to justify tyranny by some appeal to its name.

In part this longevity is due to the manifold nature of the **concept**. There have been innumerable versions of the democratic state, many of them notably undemocratic: Athenian and Roman representation, for instance, excluded slaves and women – indeed women were counted out of serious contribution to democratic government almost everywhere until the twentieth century (the first general election at which all adult women were entitled to vote in Britain was 1929). But at the heart of all democratic systems is the **principle** of self-government by a free people.

In its Athenian and then its Roman versions, such a government was placed in the hands of a *forum* of citizens whose business was to decide upon the courses of political action which would sustain the common good. In its purest version, this forum (at first, a circular theatre with raked seats where the citizens met) was intended to be open to all eligible citizens, each one equally empowered to contribute to the debate. Quickly, of course, even in a small city-state, any such practice became overwhelmed by sheer numbers, although the ideal was constantly revived by assorted revolutionary groups across history, including the English Levellers (a significant name) in the seventeenth century, the Russian Soviets in the 1920s, and Mao Zedong's Eighth Route Army before the Chinese Revolution of 1949.

The crux of modern democracy is the idea of representation and the familiar instrument of its reality is the vote. By voting for a person who will represent us in Parliament, we authorise (that is, give our authority to) that person to speak on our behalf in the political debate and to help decide what shall be done in our name. By the same token, that representative may act on our behalf to oppose the government in a variety of ways, and we revoke that representative's authority by voting him or her out of office, and a new replacement in.

Thus, the vote enacts the original principle of calling **power** to account and keeping it answerable to the popular will which is at the heart of democracy. Over the centuries, moreover, there have been repeated recreations of the capacity to act and decide together, and as societies re-imagine and re-order themselves, so they have contrived new instruments of representative voting, aspiring always to make voting into an accurate expression of mass decisions and preferences as to who will perform the work of government.

It may roughly be said that for these organisms to count as democratic, which is to say, 'rule by the people', the following conditions must hold: every citizen must vote; the representatives with most votes must win; information about candidates and policy decisions must be freely available; citizens must be well-educated and willing participants in political argument and practice; access to the institutions of information and power must be equal and open.

It is easy to see, with such a list in hand, how rarely even diminutive city-states can live up to the theoretic ideal. Democracy now seems to be the name for the good intentions of the state, something to which every society aspires but can never have. Whether or not this is the case, it is clear that like so many of our key **concepts**, democracy is at once a term identifying the facts of the matter ('such-and-such is or is not a democratic state of affairs') *and* a term of evaluation, picking out features of politics which we hold to be desirable. To say something is not democratic is to condemn it, although it is worth pointing out that until the mighty revolutions in France and America in 1789 and 1776 respectively, the word democracy was a term used with widespread disapproval for the previous half-millennium.

It is, therefore, a tricky business applying democratic **ideas** in a **school**, most of whose pupils are there under compulsion. It is, of course, important to teach democratic principles and political history, but harder to practise them in school life. Various progressive pedagogues between 1900 and 1939 started schools intended to express democratic liberties in all their aspects, notably Maria Montessori, Rudolf Steiner, Dora and Bertrand Russell, and A. S. Neill.

They had, indeed, considerable influence on state practice. School councils sometimes replaced the old prefectorial system, some aspects of school life were governed by popular voting, 'participant democracy' was appealed to as a key social **value** to be inculcated. The Quaker movement's democratic preference for gradual discussion and the slow formation of a common purpose rather than proceeding at once to a vote has been latterly aired in progressive **comprehensives**. More generally, the idea of democratic **freedom** as itself one of the virtues, formally at least, is much celebrated in everyday school life.

FURTHER READING

John Dunn (2005), *Setting the People Free: The Story of Democracy.* London: Atlantic Press.
Amy Gutmann and Denis Thompson (2004), *Why Deliberative Democracy?* Princeton: Princeton University Press.
David Held (1995), *Democracy and the Global Order.* Cambridge: Polity Press.

democracy

This is a **concept** intrinsic not just to **education** but to most human **societies** in the modern world. It constitutes a whole body of **theory** and policy studies around the application of economics in areas of poverty ('underdevelopment' is the euphemism), and in itself announces the power of the common belief in feasible **progress** central to all policy science. In this sense of 'development', the word connotes on one hand the bringing of progress by the agencies of the rich world to areas of under-development generally on the outer limits of their own wealth (areas such as the tip of Nova Scotia in Canada, of Northern Ireland in Britain, of the further corners of Sardinia untouched by tourist droppings, or the bitter, cold edges of Latvia and Estonia). On the other hand, it also refers to efforts by governments and non-governmental organisations (NGOs in the news reports) to bring progress, defined largely as economic growth, or at least as decent housing, sanitation, health care and **schools**, to those nations who have never known such things, or have lost them at the hands of tyrants and incompetents.

Development, in this now dominant meaning, is much put about just now as to whether its practitioners should simply arrive and put their plans into action (there being no one capable of acting on the spot), or whether it is better that the people who live there should learn, slowly and unevenly, to implement the policies for themselves. In this connection, the ideas of Amartya Sen about **freedom** defined as the acquisition of locally needful 'capabilities' for the successful exercise of locally practicable 'functionings' have proved their **power**.

The other, pedagogically older sense of development shares with its economic connotation the same belief in progress at the heart of the concept, and it has largely been the psychologists who have given 'development' its educational codification.

In the 1920s and 1930s, Jean Piaget, working in Switzerland often with his own children, gradually drew up a table of 'stages of cognitive development', where cognitive means, as it does, processes of mind pertaining to reasoning, thinking, problem solving, logical analysis. At the first or 'sensorimotor' stage (0 to 2 years of age), children adjust what they see, feel, hear, taste and smell to what they can do. At the second, 'pre-operational' stage (2 to 7 years), they can't use logic but they can use symbols (language, numbers, toys). At the third, 'concrete operational' stage (7 to 11 years), they begin to think logically and to reason things out, but cannot manage hypotheses or abstractions. In Piaget's best-known experiment, it is only during these years that they finally puzzle out that volumes of water stay the same when poured into glasses of different capacities. The fourth and last stage of cognitive development is the 'formal operational' (11+ years) in which abstract and systematic thought becomes possible. What most struck Piaget during a lifetime's experiment was the innate compulsion in children to make sense of the world, to make it coherent and intelligible.

Once Piaget had shown the way, theories of development became the main theme and practice of child psychology. Jerome Bruner modified and made Piaget's diagram of development more flexible as well as more responsive to cultural difference, in addition establishing just how sociable and conversational development has to be. Lawrence Kohlberg followed Piaget in drawing up, during the 1960s and by way of experiment, the sequences of *moral* development in children. Stage one is, he reckoned, oriented to punishment and obedience; stage two the assertion of egoism, the goodness of pleasure and the beginnings of sharing with others. Stage three brings expectations of the moral conduct of others, at least in small groups, the discovery of trust, loyalty and fairness; stage four the enlargement of this horizon to embrace the concepts of duty and law. Stage five lifts the **individual** to the plane of individual rights, to the discovery that **values** may change and may be disputed, as well as to the solidification of a belief in the sanctity of each person's life and liberty. At the sixth stage, the individual becomes capable of resolving his or her own ethical **principles**, of sorting between personal conscience and the law, with the former as always paramount.

Kohlberg's stages are not, as is obvious, confined to **childhood** and his model of ideal moral development is of a decidedly individualist, not to say American colour. But most **liberal**, that is, Anglophone and European teachers would endorse its outline, while wanting to qualify the exclusiveness of its categories and its rather too humourless advance to agnostic piety.

development

FURTHER READING

Jerome Bruner (1966), *Towards a Theory of Instruction*. Cambridge, MA: Harvard University Press.

Lawrence Kohlberg (1969), *Stages in the Development of Moral Thought and Action*. New York: Holt, Rinehart and Winston.

Jean Piaget (1926), *The Language and Thought of a Child*. New York: Harcourt Brace.

Amartya Sen (1999), *Development as Freedom*. Oxford: Oxford University Press.

Discipline

The word is derived from 'disciple' and originally meant 'instruction imparted to disciples or scholars'. This concept of instruction has been taken in two directions, on the one hand order maintained among pupils (which might involve correction or punishment), and on the other, a particular **subject** area or branch of **education**, as in academic discipline.

In **schools**, the word is generally used in relation to pupils' **behaviour**. This is usually of great concern to parents, who will often judge behaviour as poor on the basis of one or two incidents. Inspectors have to judge more broadly on the basis of behaviour and attitudes in lessons, pupils' behaviour towards each other, their response to school policies on managing behaviour, and any records of racist and bullying incidents.

Discipline is always a major anxiety for teachers, as once it has broken down in the classroom, no **learning** can take place. The teacher may continue **teaching**, but the learners will be causing merry mayhem amongst themselves. Many teachers feel they no longer have adequate sanctions. They are dependent on the force of their own personalities, and also the systems that operate in school. Many schools have a set scale of consequences for types of misbehaviour, so that pupils know exactly what will happen if they choose to behave in a particular way (which may be not handing in homework, or, further up the scale, calling the teacher some unpleasant names). Schools still have the right to exclude pupils, although this is often seen as a failure on the part of the school. Many schools have successful learning bases, where pupils are sent as a form of internal exclusion. These bases are run by staff who have to be skilled in behaviour **management**.

It is obviously a good thing that any kind of physical punishment is now illegal, as this would be tantamount to child abuse, and in any case teachers do not really want to run their classrooms through fear. The opposite approach is promoted in many schools. This is called 'assertive discipline', which means managing behaviour through positives – rewards for good behaviour, rather than punishment when it is poor. Assertive discipline is based on the need to respect and **value** pupils. The idea is that pupils will find it more enjoyable to be rewarded than to cause trouble. There will always be some, however, who think it is more fun to be disruptive.

discipline

It is widely believed, at the present, that school discipline is often shaky, but it is worth recalling that as recently as the early 1960s miscreants (in boys' schools) were beaten with a cane in front of the whole school and that in the 1930s school riots were not unusual affairs. The sociologist Basil Bernstein suggested that as schools and parents have reduced their powers of acculturation and loosened their systems of control, a larger realm of social **identity** is available in a pupil to be filled up by the forces of commercial **culture**. Reclaiming these zones of personal identity is difficult.

One aspect of this easing of the pressures of acculturation brings us to the other, linked meaning of a discipline as a particular form of **knowledge** and branch of learning, such as maths, physics, history, English and so forth. A discipline, **subject** or form of knowledge may be characterised as having a distinctive set of **concepts**, a singular **method**, a special idiom or linguistic register (that is, a special style and vocabulary) and, naturally, its own list of sacred books and revered practitioners.

All these attributes mark the intellectual identity of the student the longer he or she perseveres in the study. But these clear signs of a discipline are constantly on the move, are historically changeful, and readily flow across the boundaries of a subject into the next one. Thus, physics and chemistry blur together in biogenetics, sociology crosses into history and philosophy, maths is everywhere.

This confusion, sometimes exhilarating, sometimes demented, seems very marked at the present. One consequence is that the grip of subject disciplines is relaxed and in many cases is replaced by the far less definite term 'studies'. The looser, less disciplined approach this implies has the merit of open-mindedness and **freedom** of exploration but the demerit of uncertainty, immethodicality and, at the limit, a lack of any agreement about the specific knowledge belonging to the inquiry in hand.

FURTHER READING

Basil Bernstein (1975), 'Classification and framing' in his *Class, Codes and Control*, vol. 3. London: Routledge and Kegan Paul.
Fred Inglis (1985), *The Management of Ignorance*. Oxford: Basil Blackwell.

Education

Here we are at the titular **concept** of the book, everyone has an opinion about it, newspapers never leave the topic alone, yet there is remarkably little agreement both about what it is and what it ought to be. In 1997, the then prime minister, Tony Blair, famously announced as his three main priorities, 'education, education and education', and both before and since that date government policy-makers from both sides of the House of Commons have been assiduous in ensuring that education remains amenable to constant reform, and that its products – the pupils – are minutely tested, surveyed and interrogated to determine what state their education is in, and how it compares with the past.

As usual, the content of the concept is found in its uses and applications, and these are so various because *everyone* has been to **school** and been given some kind of education, hence everyone (and especially that large majority which has children) is ready with opinions and **judgements** how best to educate the next generation.

That last point is usefully definitional: a **society**'s education is that mode of more or less compulsory tutelage which shows the next generation how its parent generation believes it should move into the future by way of a present intelligibly leading out of the past. One way of envisioning the whole process is to see education as a body of narratives, each with its plot and leading characters, each with a beginning, middle and end, but where the end is less a finale and more a signpost leading onwards into time.

These narratives may most easily be made visible in the way **individual subjects** or **disciplines** are taught and learned. Thus, science teaches by example the practical rationality and **value** of methodical inquiry into and victory over the mysteries of nature. It teaches that nature may be harnessed for good or evil, and that humankind had better prefer the first. It teaches that unself-interested and detached observation is a prime **virtue** in a person. It teaches that science is a supremely important activity throughout a life, and well rewarded also. It teaches by implication that this is a story mostly for boys to learn, and that science is on the whole a boy's **career**.

Every subject tells a story, and larger than the sum of curricular narratives is the general narrative of a national education as embodied and dramatised in the everyday life of a school – in its customs, rituals, **culture** and beliefs, in its very architecture and symbols, in the demeanour and postures of staff and students.

Studied for these manifestations, school life demonstrates these things about the allegiances, commitments and errors of the whole society, its ancestors and its hopes. Indeed, one of the most illuminating pursuits into the meanings of a society's education will lead the inquirer to find the residues and deposits of the past still charging up with their energy the practical life of the present. Thus, special marks of seniority and **authority** given to the oldest pupils almost invariably carry traces of the prefectorial system invented to police boys' boarding schools for the middle classes in the nineteenth century.

Naturally, as it is a precept of this book to emphasise, the concept of education is also laden with the deposits from the thought of those many philosophers who have written about it. Plato's *Republic* was the first to argue for state and not family education (boys only), for public-spiritedness and civic-mindedness as paramount, for the centrality of character as much as the **training** of **intelligence**. Two thousand years later, Rousseau in *Emile* (1762) took it all back, and argued for a much freer, more playful and *happier* kind of education, in which the child's own **experience** and self-expressiveness would be allowed to find its own best form. In the centuries-long debate about education, one way of giving it order is to fix a fight between Plato and Rousseau.

These hundreds of cross-currents flow into the present argument, and are compounded by the insatiable demands of the global economy and the need of the society to train its children to be able to respond to them. At its crudest, an education for the future must, on the one hand, try to fulfil for students the best hopes of liberalism that they will be free, self-critical and fulfilled, and on the other, that they will have the intellectual resources, the practical training and the relevant skills to help the country pay its way and make decent living generally available.

To do this, it is possible to end by saying that a society's education should face up to and accommodate four realms of **value**: first, a respectful attitude towards nature herself, as providing the stuff of life but as not being endlessly exploitable; second, a balanced account of the past as **teaching** us what has been well or badly done, and how to do better; third, a sensible evaluation of the meaning of **work** in our lives, and what is now called the work–life balance; fourth, a shared and non-doctrinal attitude towards the death of one generation as taking its meaning from the parents' having bequeathed a sufficient and responsible prosperity and happiness to their children and, if possible, *their* children; lastly, a degree of consensus on the main individual values of the day, holding together in a single polity with a due politeness the bewildering differences of the nation's membership – local, ethnic, religious, historical.

FURTHER READING

Fred Inglis (ed.) (2004), *Education and the Good Society*. Basingstoke: Palgrave.
Alasdair MacIntyre (2006), *The Tasks of Philosophy*. Cambridge: Cambridge University Press.
R. S. Peters (1966), *Ethics and Education*. London: Allen and Unwin.
John White (1990), *Education and the Good Life: Beyond the National Curriculum*. London: Continuum.

education

Elite is another of those **concepts** (like **culture** or **identity**) which has a busy life in everyday conversation and a more specialised one in the technical vocabulary of sociology. Translated literally from the French, it simply means 'chosen' or 'elected' but even the latter term may be ambiguous, as when we refer to 'the elect' as meaning an exclusive group somehow set over or above others, as opposed to those elected to a social office by the familiar **methods** of democratic voting.

Certainly 'elites' are those groups commonly recognised as set apart and above other people by **virtue** of certain talents (for example, sporting elites), or by certain attributes (the beautiful people), or – more usually in social analysis – by the possession of the three main indices of politics: **power**, privilege and wealth. Of course, elite shades off into celebrity and the vast and mischievous industry of celebrity-spotting, adoring and denigrating is one way of studying social elites as defined by the media.

In the human sciences, elites are thought of as particular and perhaps rivalrous segments of the ruling **class**. If social classes are the joint product of economic position and cultural status, then elites form certain fractions of the upper class, and are identifiable as such either by a shared social function (as in the case of political rulers or military commanders), or by high social visibility (film or television stars), or by the sheer scale of their possessions and wealth (the international rich).

In what are called the developed economies, these different fractions of the elites may meet as celebrities in front of television cameras but hardly overlap in terms of social significance or political power. Only in periods of social upheaval and meltdown do, say, film or rock stars, footballers or intellectuals occupy a central place in political action. When the former film star (of B movies only), Ronald Reagan, became president of the USA in 1980, he only did so after two decades or more in more junior political posts.

It was in the latter part of the nineteenth century that thinkers such as Vilfredo Pareto and Gaetano Mosca, mostly arguing in opposition to Karl Marx, tried to theorise and explain the formation of elites as well as to insist that they were and are necessary to the stability of *any* **society**, as well as to that society's smaller institutions such as **schools**.

There then followed fierce debates between the egalitarians for whom elites affronted the principle of **equality** and those we might call the functionalists for whom elites are inevitable and useful.

Into this argument there burst an American sociologist, C. Wright Mills, with his thrilling book *The Power Elite*, a study of America which not only brought into view the bitter rivalry between the three dominant elites – political, corporate and military – but documented in high glee the greed, wastefulness and ignorant irresponsibility of each section of his elite trinity.

His is a caustic **judgement**, but it leaves the argument where it was as to the necessity of elites. In educational institutions, it is true, elites form themselves spontaneously, partly because amongst young people the mere process of growing up and getting stronger marks out social group membership and assigns status, partly because success in one's studies is properly rewarded and unevenly distributed, so **intelligence** and **achievement** are unstable signs of elite membership.

One abusive term in educational argument should be resisted by egalitarians and functionalists alike. It is 'elitist', generally applied to anyone who insists on important intellectual or aesthetic distinctions. These latter are essential to thought itself, and 'elitist' is then no more than the noise of a philistine's rancour. In school, the virtuous democrat and serious scholar will always seek to hold the balance between honouring the **principles** of educational merit and respecting the unevenness of human performance. It isn't easy.

FURTHER READING

T. B. Bottomore (1984), *Elites and Society*. Harmondsworth: Penguin.
C. Wright Mills (1956), *The Power Elite*. New York: Oxford University Press.

elite

Equality

For a couple of centuries or more after the French Revolution whose banners were inscribed 'liberté, egalité, fraternité', equality was a **value** at the centre of political aspiration and policy-making. More recently, its most obvious manifestation, equality of rewards and of incomes, has ceded place to the conflicting value of **individual** success and **achievement**.

As money has come to be, as never before, at once the driving force and magnetic goal of the rich **societies** like Britain and the USA, the strength of equality has faded for a while, but it is a truism that no modern society can tolerate for long such grotesque and brutal discrepancies of wealth as now are to be found in the USA (the top 1,000 chief executives in the USA command average salaries 473 times larger than the average wage of their own employees) and in Britain. The socialist political thinker R. H. Tawney proposed as long ago as 1931 that no income in society should be more than 10 times greater than the lowest income, and this takes the measure of the strength of equality as a **concept** at that date.

The concept seems to have two aspects, not necessarily at odds. It starts out from the plain fact that human beings are equal in being commonly human. This platitude runs immediately into the no less plain fact that all humans are *un*equally equipped with their attributes – their physique, intelligence, health, capabilities, **virtues** and so forth. While this is of course true, nonetheless there is **power** in the original truism, as the American Declaration of Independence reminds us: 'We hold these **truths** to be self-evident … that all men are created equal'. It has been a great advance in our sense of what is due to the ideal of equality that nobody now would fail to add 'and women' to the Declaration.

In matters of equality of treatment of others, everything turns on its application. Here it is simplest to gather all considerations, as remarked, under two headings: equality of opportunity and equality of respect. The first is commonly acknowledged as a strong political **value**; the second is formally paid tribute but hugely disregarded, most obviously in the scales of monetary rewards (which provide, after all, the readiest measure of respect).

Equality of opportunity is generally taken to mean opportunity to make one's own way in the world without unequal or unjust obstacles to oneself or advantages to others. **Education** is perhaps the most obvious place for its application, and certainly all **schools** try to observe its value. In doing so, systems of education should have regard to two obvious *in*equalities which will weigh upon policies intended to equalise opportunity: of need and of merit. So deprived children need more attention than better-off children in the name of attaining equality of opportunity; all pupils shall have, for instance, equality of access to a university education, but not all have the merit or talents. Finally, equality of opportunity must of necessity also be limited by the nature of the goods one is to have an opportunity to sample. Everybody shall have such equality, say, to attend special dance classes after school. But access will not only be limited by merit ('Are you any good at dancing?') but by scope. When the class is full, the list is closed.

It was in the name of equality of opportunity that (almost all) grammar schools were abolished. **Comprehensive** education was and is an admirable attempt to institutionalise *both* forms of equality. Setting aside the notable historical success of comprehensive schools in defending equality, it should be said that upholding equality of respect is, as it should be, a genuine value present in almost all schools. To think of it as a mere platitude is to overlook the monstrous inequalities of respect which issue, worldwide, in terrible wounds both moral and physical. Of course, equality of respect is only due to those people and their beliefs which deserve respect and are respectable. It is not to be awarded blindly.

FURTHER READING

Tony Judt (2005), *Postwar: a History of Europe since 1945*. London: Penguin.
Thomas Nagel (1991), *Equality and Patriarchy*. New York: Oxford University Press.
R. H. Tawney (1931), *Equality*. London: Allen and Unwin.
Bernard Williams (1973), 'Equality', in *Problems of the Self*. Cambridge: Cambridge University Press.

equality

Examination

'Examination' implies a detailed scrutiny of an object, usually involving a microscope. In school examinations, it is the pupil who is under scrutiny. At the conclusion of a course of study, the final examination determines how much the pupil has learnt; or at least, how much he or she can regurgitate in the time allowed.

In **schools**, examinations are usually referred to in the abbreviation 'exams'. They take place at the end of a course, or, in the case of a modular exam, at the end of a chunk of the course. Continuous **assessment** is a different **concept** to a final exam, as it takes place during the course and can be based, for example, on a pupil's contribution in lessons.

National tests in England at age 11 and 14 take the form of exams. These do not happen in Scotland, and the testing of pupils up to 14 years has been phased out in Wales, to be replaced by teacher assessments and a '**skills** test'. In England, results at 11, 14 and at 16 are put into 'league tables'. In their raw form, these are designed to show which schools are top dogs, and which are bottom of the pile.

Pupils in Wales take GCSE (General Certificate of Secondary **Education**), but league tables have been abolished. The system in Scotland is altogether different. Pupils there take 'Standard Grade' at age 15–16, normally in eight **subjects**, including compulsory exams in English, mathematics, a foreign language, a science subject and a social subject. After Standard Grade, students can choose to remain at school to study for Access, Intermediate or Higher Grade. Some stay on for a further year to take Advanced Higher exams. Entry to Scottish universities can take place with Higher Grade qualifications.

In England and Wales, pupils take GCSE exams, usually in Year 11 when they are 16 (although children born in July or August will still be 15). Some schools enter some pupils earlier in selected subjects. Students who go into the sixth form take AS level in Year 12 and A2 in Year 13. The only compulsory subjects at GCSE are English, mathematics and science. Some pupils take 11 or 12 subjects altogether.

The picture is further complicated by the fact that different syllabuses are offered by different exam boards. Syllabuses have to fit in with national specifications, but the exam boards are commercial organisations and are obviously keen to tailor their syllabuses, and forms of examination, to make them more attractive to schools. There is now a greater number of modular exams, and testing online.

Currently there are complaints that exams are getting easier, and various newspapers make comparisons between O levels (which were phased out in the 1980s) and GCSE, and between old A levels and A2 levels. This is pointless, as the exams have different purposes. In the 1960s, only 7 per cent of the population went to university, and it was important that one of the things exams did was identify the most academic children. Now that the government wants 50 per cent of the age group to go to university, the net has to be cast much wider. Exams are now required to be more flexible, and to test skills which are transferable.

New qualifications that are being developed emphasise this flexibility, for example, vocational diplomas. The foundation diploma is meant to be equivalent to five GCSEs, the higher diploma seven GCSEs, and the advanced diploma three A levels. Ed Balls, minister for the department of children, schools and families, said in October 2007:

> Diplomas will open up real opportunities for combining academic and practical options to allow every young person to make the most of their talents, whether they are progressing to further study, work or an apprenticeship. ... I believe that diplomas could emerge as the jewel of our education system.

There has been pressure to make A levels more flexible, more in line with the International Baccalaureate. In Wales, A levels are being phased out gradually from September 2007, to be replaced by the Welsh Baccalaureate. In England, A levels remain, but the new diplomas may prove to be more popular.

FURTHER READING

Qualifications and Curriculum Authority: www.qca.org.uk

examination

Excellence

To excel is, of course, to be the best, or among the best. It is possible to excel in something evil, as Henry V says to one of the traitors:

> And whatsoever cunning fiend it was
> That wrought upon thee so preposterously
> Hath got the voice in hell for excellence … (Act 2, Scene 2)

Schools aspire to be excellent, or, in the current Ofsted parlance, 'outstanding'. It helps when results in tests or **examinations** are well above the national average, but a school can still be outstanding with lower results, if it can be shown that pupils have made exceptional **progress** from the time they entered the school. This is usually demonstrated by 'CVA' (contextual **value** added). A school would have to be in at least the top 20 per cent to be given grade 1. In a special school, evidence of progress will be shown on an **individual** basis.

Teachers aspire to teach outstanding lessons, in which all pupils are fully engaged, enjoying themselves and making 'exceptionally good progress'. Pupils aim for the highest grades in order to achieve excellence. At one time, a grade A was excellence at GCSE, but as the numbers reaching A increased, A* was introduced. Now a super A* is proposed, and similar changes are in the pipeline for A level, in order to identify an **elite** in the top 1 per cent.

In the relentless drive to classify all schools, some that are outstanding are designated 'beacon schools' or 'centres of excellence', the **idea** being that they should share their good practice with other schools. At least this encourages collaboration, rather than competition between institutions.

FURTHER READING

www.standards.dcsf.gov.uk/beaconschools

Experience

This is one of the most frequently invoked honorifics in the everyday **language** of **pedagogy**. To learn from experience and to ground aspects of the **curriculum** in experience is to be doing the right thing and to be avoiding 'chalk and talk' (as people used to say), or – which is also thought to be both ineffectual as well as boring – 'learning by rote'.

Experience, however, turns out to be a multiple term. In its simplest version, people generally mean by it direct, lived or observed knowledge of the world. Even then, to equate experience with **knowledge** doesn't quite cover all usages: experience can be taken not so much to mean knowledge in the sense of facts about the world which one can recognise and enumerate, as distinct from mere beliefs in that they are known to be the case. Instead, experience is also understood as an accumulation of all that happens to a **person**, which then frames and directs one's actions without one's necessarily being aware of it.

There are, therefore, gradations in the degree of one's experience: to watch something happening – a battle, say, or a fierce storm – is not the same kind of experience as taking part in military action or being in a boat at sea in such a storm. In such a comparison, people typically suppose that the nearer and more immediate experience is the most significant one; this is not necessarily the case. The sailor in the boat, swamped by the sea and at his wits' end, may be so overwhelmed by the experience that he cannot at all understand it. For him, we might say, the event has never been turned by consciousness and reflection into experience.

When this happens, it may well be the case that experience yields either no knowledge at all, or that the person with the experience mistakes it and may (frequently does) use the experience as foundation for entirely erroneous or superstitious beliefs. There is then a tricky argument to have as to whether or not experience implies a content that is true or false. That is to say, can one say of an experience that it teaches a proposition? If so, then the proposition can be checked as either true or false. If not (and that is mostly how people think about experience), that is, if it doesn't have a true or false content, then how can we base beliefs on it? If experiences are then not the grounds of belief, they can't provide reasons for the world's seeming to be as it is.

These misgivings remain at the heart of the **concept**, even though teachers go on blithely trusting to experience as confirming what they teach, just as their superiors blithely suppose that in making staff appointments, experience is everything even though it is obvious that there are plenty of people who never 'learn from experience'; experience of itself guarantees nothing except the passage of time. It is only useful and usable when the possessor of the experience has the **intelligence** to understand and apply it. This can only happen when experience is gathered into a **tradition** of thought whose **principles** of rationality and the feelings these direct teach what to do with experience.

The mighty poet T. S. Eliot wrote in his poem *East Coker*:

There is, it seems to us,
At best only a limited value
In the knowledge derived from experience.
The knowledge imposes a pattern, and falsifies ...

It is probably right that teachers seek to ground their **teaching** in the pupil's experience; that way, the natural rhythms of absorption and **attention**, the reassurance of personal contact between teacher and pupil, the active movement of cognition, will work together to make learning more possible and the results worthwhile. But it isn't clear that in this process 'experience' is any more than a handy catch-all term, when what matters is a rather more careful analysis of the different presences and purposes which go to make up learning.

FURTHER READING

Martin Amis (2000), *Experience*. London: Jonathan Cape.
John Dewey (1934), *Art as Experience*. Cambridge, MA: Harvard University Press.
D. W. Hamlin (1978), *Experience and the Growth of Understanding*. London: Routledge.
Stefan Korner (1966), *Theory and Experience*. Cambridge: Cambridge University Press.

key concepts in education

Freedom

Freedom is, as everybody knows, one of the greatest and most noble of our own political ideals, but also of the commonly cherished ideals of most of the nation-states of the world. Nonetheless, it is sometimes a difficult **idea** to fill with any content, since freedom connotes an unspecific state of being in which one can do what one likes. The grim philosopher, Thomas Hobbes, who considered freedom largely a delusion, wrote in his study of the state and its sovereignty, *Leviathan* (1651), that all that is required for someone to be free is that action proceed from a person's will. Since he held a very low view of human wilfulness, it followed that freedom had better be strongly constrained by civil law and the sovereign, and that an obligation to reasonable rule will then countermand the breezy inclination to do as one wants.

Hobbes, however, is only one, if the greatest, of theoreticians of liberty in the **traditions** of political **theory**. The historian Alan Macfarlane has argued that the **concept** of freedom as the paramount political ideal made an early appearance in English legislation, and that the legal figure known as 'the freeborn Englishman' may be found standing up for his legal and human **rights** as early as the thirteenth century. Certainly the popular old narrative has it that the Magna Carta, signed by King John in 1216, was a notable victory for freedom against the autarchy of the King, and legal records in the north country during the next century indicate that some laws at least explicitly circumscribed tyranny, permitted hunting on common land (a right steadfastly fought for and upheld until common lands disappeared into the enclosures of the late eighteenth century), and forbade arbitrary arrest and feudal privilege.

Like all the most powerful and longest-lived names of political ideals, liberty mutated across the centuries. Hobbes's argument was directed to the English Revolution of the 1640s. When the eighteenth century revolutionaries in France in 1789 and America in 1776 addressed the concept, in France they were principally concerned with the destruction of the *ancien régime* and the establishment of a People's Assembly, while the Founding Fathers of the United States were, first, concerned to throw off colonial rule from Britain, and, second, to issue a rousing declaration of the 'self-evident **truth** that all men are created free' and that everyone has a right to 'life, liberty and the pursuit of happiness' (none of these happy certainties extending as far as the black slaves, or even, on the whole, to the lives of women and children).

The beginning of the nineteenth century, one could say, is the moment at which liberalism begins its canonisation of freedom as the prime **value** of politics, and freedom, as understood in Isaiah Berlin's neat formula, as *freedom from* the interference of others, especially the state, and *freedom to* do as one wants, as long as one doesn't thereby curtail the freedom of others.

This highly individualised account of freedom struck root everywhere. Such a picture of freedom was at once intelligible and attractive, at least for those **societies** likely to be able to provide enough wealth and leisure to go round. Accordingly, freedom gradually turned into freedoms of **choice** in the consumer society, which while it lasted was a happy enough indulgence, but took no account of the self-**discipline** and watchfulness required to maintain freedoms of more communal kinds. Only recently, Quentin Skinner has suggested that for freedom to be real, citizens must take part in their own government, and commended the example of Australia where, in a telling example, the electorate is compelled by law to vote, an instance of being forced to look after the condition of being free.

All this history swirls about a classroom and the many appeals made there to the necessity for freedom in **education**. At first sight, this looks contradictory, for after all, pupils are compelled by law to attend **school** (unless officially receiving education at home). But if, as many theorists claim, being free is something innate to humankind, then devising classroom conventions and curricular discipline which, so far as possible, express and encourage freedoms – of thought, activity, expression and so forth – is no more than to teach pupils how to attain a more fulfilled humanity. Moreover, freedom to become the best person it is in you to become is itself, on modern reckoning, a condition of **virtue**. To be self-reliant, independent-minded, self-critical, self-aware, self-possessed and self-assured is to be on the way to being good, as well as being in a free state.

Naturally, coercion and discipline must have their unignorable place in classrooms. Perhaps the Nobel economist, Amartya Sen, is a help to the teacher at this point. Because he sees plainly that conventional **ideas** of freedom are irrelevant to the poorer nations, he proposes an ideal of freedom attainable by the **development** and education of those *capabilities* a person has which may be expressible in the *functionings* that society makes possible.

Teachers can surely use this idea, judging the 'capabilities' of those in front of them, and matching them to 'functionings' (not only jobs but places, roles, attitudes, activities, feelings) which are there for practical application in our society.

Thus, they help their pupils towards their own, recognisable version of freedom. It then goes without saying that the classroom must embody such freedoms in its daily life, and such a prospect is perfectly compatible with the order, peacefulness and good manners indispensable to **teaching** and **learning**.

FURTHER READING

Isaiah Berlin (1969), *Four Essays on Liberty*. Oxford: Oxford University Press.

John Stuart Mill (1991 [1874]), *On Liberty and Other Essays*. Oxford: Oxford University Press.

Amartya Sen (2002), *Rationality and Freedom*. Cambridge, MA: Belknap Press.

Quentin Skinner (1997), *Liberty Before Liberalism*. Cambridge: Cambridge University Press.

freedom

Gender

The word is from the Latin *generare*, to beget, and the noun *genus*, which is a race or breed. In English, there is the verb 'to engender'. The term 'gender' itself means the sex of a person or animal, but it is a more euphemistic word than 'sex'. It is used as a grammatical term when **learning languages,** such as French or Spanish in which all nouns (not just living creatures) are masculine or feminine.

It became, however, an important term in the necessary polemics which accompanied the strong revival of feminism which began in the 1970s. The intellectual feminist judged it important to distinguish between sex, which was a largely biological term, and gender, which represented the sexual differentiation produced by **culture**.

Gender has always been an important determining factor in **education**, along with **class**. In earlier times, it was not considered important to educate girls, so gender defined their opportunities. For most of the twentieth century, the **curriculum** was different for boys and girls, chiefly in the area now called 'design and technology', with girls being directed to domestic **subjects**, and boys to woodwork or metalwork. Such overt stereotyping does not exist any more, and girls are free to choose 'resistant materials' and boys to choose 'food technology' or 'textiles' – whether they do so or not is up to them.

Once girls started to have the same educational opportunities, they proceeded to outstrip boys in terms of results. At GCSE, there is a gap of around 10 percentage points between boys' and girls' attainment, measured by five subjects at A*–C. There has been little variation in this gap for a decade, in spite of numerous projects focusing on boys' **achievement**. The largest gender differences are in the **humanities** (such as history and religious studies, as well as English language and literature), the **arts** and languages. There are smaller gender differences in science and mathematics, although girls are still ahead. Attainment at each end of the distribution of grades also varies by gender. Girls are more likely than boys to gain an A* grade at GCSE. Boys are a little more likely to gain a G grade at GCSE or to gain no GCSEs at all.

It is not surprising that girls perform better in subjects that are language-based with an emphasis on essay-writing. Their language **skills** develop earlier, and they are more likely to perform better than boys on tasks which involve open-ended writing, particularly when this involves a personal response. Boys prefer writing shorter answers. In narrative writing, most boys prefer to tell a story directly and succinctly, without much description or exploration of a character's feelings.

Because of this, the style of **examinations** has been blamed for the gender gap, especially the use of coursework. However, when the coursework component in GCSE was reduced, results from these new specifications from 1994 onwards showed that the gender gap increased.

There is a gender difference in students' **choices**, especially post-16:

Girls' most popular subject is English, while boys' is maths. Psychology, Art and Design, Sociology and Media/Film/Television Studies are amongst the 10 most popular choices for girls (but not boys), while Physics, Business Studies, Geography and Physical Education are in the top 10 for boys (but not girls). (Information taken from DfES report *Gender and Education*, 2007).

FURTHER READING

Annette Baier (1995), *Moral Prejudices*. Cambridge, MA: Harvard University Press.
Germaine Greer (1971), *The Female Eunuch*. London: Paladin.
June Hannam (2007), *Feminism*. Harlow: Pearson Education.
Mary Holmes (2007), *What is Gender? Sociological Approaches*. London: Sage.
Genevieve Lloyd (1984), *The Man of Reason: Male and Female in Western Philosophy*. London: Methuen.
Catherine MacKinnon (1995), *Feminism Unmodified: Discourses on Life and Law*. Cambridge, MA: Harvard University Press.

gender

The humanities are grouped together in a set of academic **disciplines** or **subjects** set against the natural sciences as being the separate study of non-human but physical reality. The term is an Anglicisation of the degree course, founded in Oxford in the early sixteenth century and known as *Litterae Humaniores*. By this was meant the **learning** associated with human **culture** such as grammar, rhetoric, and particularly the poetry and prose of the Latin and Greek classics, grammar, rhetoric, logic (the *trivium*).

The degree courses of this title, at Oxford and at some of the ancient Scottish universities, continued to refer to the study of Latin and Greek classics. But by 1605, when Francis Bacon published his mammoth study of all the disciplines, *The Advancement of Learning*, the word humanities was used to mark off the field of study of human conduct from 'Divine Philosophie' (theology) and 'Natural Philosophie' (or science).

The term has always been a loose one and, as the **authority** of religion weakened, theology moved to a position half in and half independent of the humanities, which meanwhile remained confident of including history, literature, the **arts** – whether practically or theoretically studied, politics and philosophy. With the advent of the new social sciences, economics, sociology and psychology in the nineteenth century, a big upheaval in the territory of **knowledge** impended, as such figures of Auguste Comte and James Mill (John Stuart Mill's father) arrived to claim that the factual and numerical study of **society** would turn the study of humankind into a proper science, and the battle was joined for the ultimate **truths** about life between the positivist scientists and the humanist *literati*.

That battle is still inconclusive. Its weapons are still fired off in the struggle between qualitative and quantitative **method**, and between subjective and **objective** reports. **Individual** subjects such as history and politics fought comparable civil wars on their own territory and meanwhile the big subject zones of humanities and sciences gathered to themselves certain of the key **values** attributed to and embodied in the study of their self-defining topics, literature and leading thinkers.

Thus, the sciences, during the period of their overwhelming dominance (roughly 1600 to 1950), represented themselves to themselves as custodians of objective method, as keepers of public (because scientific) reason, as master of nature, and as the most deserving recipients of any spare resources allocated by the State to expensive inquiry into nature (not to mention the looked-for profits from such inquiry). Since science, as so defined and practised, was both successful and powerful, it was and remains a largely masculine domain.

The humanities, in competition with this ideological world view, set themselves from the mid-nineteenth century on to be the custodians of human fulfilment and emancipation, to cherish the supposedly non-scientific properties of **imagination** and feeling, to celebrate – as so much new literature, written by women, described – the realm of private life and its key values of love (and being in love) and nurture. Thus, the humanities, especially the core disciplines of world art, music and literature, drew disproportionately from the women who entered higher and further **education** in increasing numbers after World War I.

The social sciences kept themselves to themselves by way of borrowing the prestige of science proper. The French attempted to solve the dispute with a new, useful category, the human sciences, returning, as it did, to science in its older sense as knowledge itself. The quarrel and the struggle for dominance between the humanities and the sciences goes on unabated, although it should be noted that the critics of positivism, still very much a minority, have made substantial inroads over the past several decades.

FURTHER READING

Matthew Arnold (1990[1869]), *Culture and Anarchy*, edited by S. Collini. Cambridge: Cambridge University Press.

Richard Bernstein (1975), *The Restructuring of Social Theory*. Philadelphia: University of Pennsylvania Press.

Richard Hoggart (1958), *The Uses of Literacy*. Harmondsworth: Penguin.

Fred Inglis (2004), *Culture*. Cambridge: Polity Press.

Raymond Williams (1959), *Culture and Society*. London: Chatto and Windus.

humanities

There are rather too many senses of this word in the **language** of class-rooms, and it would be as well to ration them. Back at the beginning of philosophy, Plato suggested that the ideas (or 'the Forms') existed apart from any conscious beings, and were those defining entities of **mind** which, without any location, provided the perfect shapes of thought and being towards which human beings aspired but of which they could only see the flickering and unstable shadows. (This is Plato's famous metaphor of 'the cave'.)

With the more or less modern **theories** of psychology and **knowledge** which begin in the seventeenth century, Plato's ideas were turned into something mental, and 'idea' was the name for any object of which one was conscious; this led theorists, such as Descartes and John Locke, to suppose that ideas are the content of **experience**. That is to say, I see an object out there, but because I see it in different aspects as I move or as I am shortsighted or as the light changes, what I am seeing is my idea of it, not the object itself (which doesn't change).

For a long while, therefore, ideas were largely discussed as caused by (and not really distinguishable from) our perceptions of the world. To have an idea was to have a mental image of an object. This gradually gave rise to the so-called doctrine of idealism, meaning not the pursuit of high moral ideals (which is what the word means in ordinary usage) but the contention that our ideas of the world are the only things we can be sure of, and that therefore the world *is* our idea of it. Reality is confined to the contents of our minds.

This was most strongly argued by Bishop Berkeley in the eighteenth century, who wrote that 'to be is to be perceived', and for a long time after him the philosophical doctrine of idealism held sway. The correct account of the relations between appearance and reality was clinched by the great German philosopher Hegel, who argued that consciousness of reality cannot be separated from reality itself, and that the world simply *is* human and collective self-consciousness on the way to self-knowledge. Although not many people talk like Hegel now, they may well retain something in common with the notion that **individuals** create the collective world by their 'inter-subjective' **understanding** of it, and that this collective creation is progressive.

Gradually through the nineteenth century, a rival sense of idealism as meaning a theory of **society** created in terms of its dominant ideas, came into conflict with *materialism*, especially as propounded by Karl Marx, and his revolutionary idea ('standing Hegel on his head' as he put it) that society is driven and changed by its economic and not its idealist structures. Ruling ideas – such as liberty or individuality – are, Marx said, simply high-minded disguise wrapped around the engines of **power** and privilege by the ruling **classes**.

'Idea', therefore, carries multiple charges even in its most commonplace appearance. Mostly, 'to have a good idea' seems only to indicate a happy novelty in one's thought, but whatever the context, there will be hidden in it an assumption about what an idea really is: it may be a mental image of a perception; it may be a phenomenon of consciousness as it sorts itself out with regard to an object; it may be a sudden movement of the imagination linking or explaining or interpreting something in a new way; it may be a slow compilation of meanings arrived at by a whole society, as in the idea of nature or of history or of God. Whichever of these (and plenty more) the word indicates, there will lie behind it theoretic presuppositions about the making of minds and of the world.

FURTHER READING

Simon Blackburn (1999), *Think*. Oxford: Oxford University Press.
R. G. Collingwood (1946), *The Idea of History*. Oxford: Oxford University Press.
Liam Hudson (1968), *Frames of Mind*. Cambridge: Cambridge University Press.
Bertrand Russell (1912), *The Problems of Philosophy*. Oxford: Oxford University Press.

idea

93

Identity, one would think, is one **concept** everybody should be clear about. One's own identity being that configuration of attributes and inheritance which make one who one really is and not somebody else, then the expectation would surely be that the components of identity would be as hard and definite as stone. This expectation would be the stronger for identity's having become the source in contemporary political argument of so much fierce self-assertion and displays, even murderous ones, of invincible self-righteousness.

One possible explanation for the heat and hatred engendered by identity disputes may well be the widespread ruptures and dissolution of natural ties to families, neighbourhoods, ethnic groups and nations which have been effected by the vast economic changes generalised as globalisation. It may be exactly this instability which makes people affirm an identity menaced by loss or even destruction. At such a time, when the fixtures and safeties of one's being and belonging begin to break up, a person holds all the tighter to what he or she believes to be ultimate allegiances, or alternatively, searches in the debris of historical upheaval for signs or souvenirs to hang onto.

In this process one may discern three strands of meaning which each **individual** seeks to twist together into the rope of identity. The first such strand ties a **person**, so to say, to a moral horizon; it is by way of my identity that I know what is truly important to me, it positions me in social and moral space. Thus, I learn such a position from what is *given* about me – my race, my social **class**, my family and the duties I have towards it, my age, character, **intelligence** and so forth.

However, as soon as somebody compiles such a list, it is obvious that many of these quantities are not at all given. I may come to detest being bound by some of them and vow to myself that I simply cannot adhere, say, to my inherited religion. Identity is therefore not only what is given, it is also what is accepted, chosen at some deep level of allegiance. It is personal. It is what I can, in a powerful phrase, feel at home with and in. It is what permits me to feel authentic and to be sincere (both key terms in modern ethics). The difficulty is then to be recognised by others in this personal **choice**, for such choice is invalidated if it is not accorded social recognition. Hence the importance of the struggle for recognition by groups once derided or ignored for, say, their racial origins or sexual orientations.

The two strands of identity – the given and the personally chosen – are then joined by a third more or less compulsory element, which is that for the given and the chosen to possess social reality they must bind together individual identities into a joint social actor. That is to say, identity must be capable, to count as social reality, of effective social action. For example, my inheritance may appoint me a huntsman, my personal allegiance to hunting may corroborate my inheritance, but unless there are hunts for me to join, my identity is broken off and cannot be fulfilled.

We can begin to see by now why identity is inherently contentious in modern **society**. If you want to hold hard to the old ways in a new world, you will have to change your way of being traditional in the very act of fighting to defend it. So it is that identity is attached to the powerful related **value** of human dignity. In a more or less egalitarian present, one's acknowledged dignity as a person and a citizen confirms one's identity (hence the force of the protest, 'Treat me as a person!'). Identity is one name for self-worth, and it will prove a lifetime's task to define this; identity may be thought of as the taking shape of a satisfactory life history.

FURTHER READING

Luce Iragaray (1985), *An Ethics of Sexual Difference*. Ithaca: Cornell University Press.
Amelie Rorty (ed.) (1982), *Identities of Persons*. San Francisco: University of California Press.
Amartya Sen (2006), *Identity and Violence*. Cambridge, MA: Harvard University Press.
Bernard Williams (1973), *Problems of the Self*. Cambridge: Cambridge University Press.

identity

Ideology

Ideology started life, like so many of our political **concepts**, in the Enlightenment and during the French Revolution. It then meant no more than a system of (probably recent) **ideas**. However, it quickly took on a slightly fishy-smelling suggestion, as exemplified in the joke conjugation: 'I have wisdom and **experience**; you have beliefs; he has an ideology'. By now, indeed, ideology itself has been thoroughly ideologised, which is to say has been turned into an object of ideological dispute as between holders of different sets of ideological opinions.

It was Karl Marx and Friedrich Engels who started it, and turned the concept into so bristling a landmine. In *The German Ideology*, written during 1848, the year of widespread revolution in Europe, they argued that the ruling ideas of an epoch are no more than the ideas of a ruling **class** justifying and expressing its political and economic dominance. At the same time, Marx and Engels insisted that when men argue about ideas in this way they remain wholly unaware of self-interest and partisanship. Thus, when the good **liberal** commends **freedom** of trade, individuality of **development** and independence of thought, he (and Marx and Engels were thinking only about men) had no consciousness of how these doctrines suited his private advantages but not those workers whose only weapons of resistance were collective.

Thus was devised what might be called the 'fix' **theory** of ideology. By its lights, ideologies are instruments with which to deceive everybody including oneself, to sustain a condition of 'false consciousness' (Engels's phrase) according to which one's high ideals were not self-serving hypocrisy but the common aspiration of all. Belief was thus socially grounded in class **structure**.

Once people learned this lesson, they were quick to pounce on its many manifestations. For it is intrinsic to the theory of **society** or of moral conduct (the realms, respectively, of sociology, political science and ethics) that one judges how things are against how they ought to be. This being so, all preferences are open to accusation from their critics as being ideological, or the product of schemes of ideas with unnoticed partisanship written deep in their premises. Even the unrealisable ideal of scientific objectivity in social inquiry is accused of its own special ideological bias.

By this way of thinking, ideology is a mask to conceal reality rather than a portrait to reveal it. A more recent thinker, Clifford Geertz, proposes that ideology may be differently criticised not as a political fix but as a way of taking the strain of life. In 'strain theory', ideology takes the strain of the big discrepancies in social life, not only giving a supportive explanation of the chronic malintegration of society, the juddering collisions of profitability with happiness for example; it also provides solace for the severe wounds inflicted on the **individual** by these shocks and brutal accidents. Ideology then offers to hold in a single, sufficiently plausible vision the grimness of the actual world and the hope of how it might be made better.

Ideology has therefore a vital emotional function. It softens or hardens, succours or exasperates one's feelings about the feasibility of action. But a more ambitious account of ideology, also propounded by Geertz, has it that we shall best understand its working by treating it as 'a constellation of enshrined ideas'. To understand ideology in action, in other words, we should see it as a publicly enacted drama, and by analysing its tropes, its rhetoric, its gestures and scenery, its forms of characterisation and its conception of plot – analysing therefore the whole style of its dramaturgy – we shall be able to grasp both its delusive magic and its reassuring rationality. For when **culture** and practice let you down, ideology will see you through.

Such analysis is easy to envisage in a **school**. Consider its rituals, its boundaries (between ages, **subjects**, sexes, **work** and play), its **language**, its displays, its laws and dress, and you can tell the story of its dramatised meanings and thereby its ideology.

FURTHER READING

Terry Eagleton (1991), *Ideology: An Introduction*. London: Verso.
Clifford Geertz (1995), 'Ideology as a Cultural System' in *The Interpretation of Cultures*. London: Hutchinson.
Karl Mannheim (1936), *Ideology and Utopia*. London: Routledge and Kegan Paul.
John Plamenatz (1970), *Ideology*. London: Macmillan.

ideology

This is one of the most powerful honorifics in the vocabulary of **teaching**, yet everybody would be hard put to say what it is and how we know when we are using it. Still harder is to say whether or not the imagination can be exercised by use or improved by some kind of **training**. Nonetheless, most of us as parents or teachers believe that in giving children time and space to 'use their imaginations' (generally in the practice of one of the **arts**) they are doing something right and important.

Stripped down, the imagination is the faculty of **mind** which permits thought about things either not present to the senses or not real at all, although these processes may be hard to tell apart from ordinary remembering. But deploying one's imagination (and whatever it is, is very hard to control) leads a person into very varied forms of thought. At times the imagination works in more or less vivid mental images, as when you imagine yourself paddling a canoe up the Amazon. Even then, Jean-Paul Sartre reminds us, the imagination only provides you with enough for the story, not everything you would see if you were there. In reading a novel in which two characters are talking in a room, you don't usually imagine the details of furniture or clothing or even the timbre of their voices, but make do with minimum scenery and sound effects.

At other times, the imagination can work with imagined possibilities and without any imagery at all, as when imagining an abstract change in one's **society** – alterations in the legal status of immigrants, say.

Either way it seems to be true that it is the visual and auditory imagination which are strongest; it is more difficult to imagine smells or tastes than pictures or sounds. What is not in doubt is that in imagining a person is acting freely, and this recognition is why in **education** so much is made of the imagination as a token of **individuals** as belonging to themselves. When, moreover, we see the poverty of imaginative life in those who have experienced little imaginative exercise, and observe the clichés and banality of so much popular narrative (video games, for instance), then it seems likely that the free imagining encouraged by the best literature is indeed a necessary part of education and will indeed have beneficial effects.

All the same, teachers should guard against supposing that free imagining is of itself morally admirable. Plenty of people have proved themselves horribly imaginative in the devising of tortures or retribution. Nor should it be thought that the imagination is at its best when practising the arts. Particle physics and its near relations cosmology and astronomy have made their extraordinary advances of the past century and a half by highly imaginative postulation of unproved conditions and entities. The famous 'black holes' of space where gravity is absolute and light extinguished had to be imagined before they were discovered. Einstein's and Planck's running together of space and time, when these had always been believed to be fundamentally distinct, was an imaginative thunderbolt.

All the same, the arts have strong claims to be the most active realm of the imagination, especially in literature and the imagining of narrative. It is surely important, as every teacher recognises, to encourage children in what in any case comes naturally to them, and have them play out those fictional narratives in which they can experiment with being other people and try out the powerful notion of human difference before coming safely home to bed.

More than this, however, it is the imagination which, in the arts for sure but also all the time in everyday life, orders our vision and **experience** into an intelligible and significant whole. Mysterious it certainly is, but there are good grounds for thinking of the imagination as the supreme faculty of mind.

FURTHER READING

R. G. Collingwood (1938), *The Principles of Art*. Oxford: Oxford University Press.
Jean-Paul Sartre (1972), *The Psychology of Imagination*. London: Methuen.
Lionel Trilling (1950), *The Liberal Imagination*. London: Heinemann.
Mary Warnock (1973), *Imagination*. Oxford: Oxford University Press.

imagination

The word 'inclusion' obviously comes from 'include', and signifies the act of including. Its significance arises from **questions** of treatment according to the **value** of **equality**. In educational terms, it is the opposite of 'exclusion' – instead of trying to get rid of difficult or problematic youngsters, it means including all types of learners, whatever their background, difficulties or disabilities.

Many **schools** are still 'exclusive', especially selective schools, which do not admit those pupils who are unlikely to reach high standards. Specialist schools are able to select at least a proportion of their intake on the basis of aptitude for their particular specialism. 'Faith' schools admit pupils mainly on the basis of their parents' religious allegiance.

A truly inclusive school would not set criteria of this sort, but would meet the needs of the whole range of pupils, including those with **learning** difficulties and disabilities. However, pupils with the severest disabilities need special facilities, and realistically have to attend schools which can provide these resources.

Schools are expected to have policies which demonstrate inclusiveness. They should be able to show how they work with vulnerable children and pupils at risk of exclusion to keep them in school. They must monitor the **achievement** of all children to make sure that they are progressing at least as well as would be expected, including pupils from various ethnic minorities, and pupils with specific difficulties and disabilities. In this way, no one should be excluded from the opportunities offered in school.

This is all part of what is called the Every Child Matters agenda (ECM), in which the emphasis is on 'every'. Schools have a **responsibility** to promote the 'five outcomes' of ECM. These are to ensure that all children are enabled to be healthy; stay safe; enjoy and achieve; make a positive contribution; achieve economic well-being.

There is a clash between a school's wish to be inclusive, and its desire to reach higher **standards**. Admitting certain pupils might depress results. This is described well in the report *Equity in Education*:

> The report demonstrates how mechanisms of **choice** and competition which are central to current policies, at best reproduce existing social divisions, and at worst may exacerbate these. It shows how, rather than

promoting a diverse range of educational provision, competition between schools and colleges has led to the narrowing of educational opportunities, as they seek to attract the most academically able learners, and to maintain or raise their local status according to government **targets**. At the same time, it encourages the growth of dubious practices to exclude the most vulnerable. (University of Manchester, January 2007)

inclusion

This is one of the most important political and moral categories in the language. But before touching on its well-known (but much argued-over) usages, it is necessary to indicate a more technical use where the term means simply *one* of something. For our purposes, it is worth noting that the ways we have of identifying something as strictly individual (that is, unique) are often rough and ready, and that scientific **method** in particular must be at pains to be as certain as possible when it has discovered an individual (which therefore cannot be an example nor a **class**, still less a genus or species).

Individuals in the conventional sense are similarly just that: each of us is the only one, the single instantiation of you or me, and this is a sufficiently frightening **idea**. The word therefore carries an instantaneous moral force, as in the idea of individual **responsibility**, individual **choice** or of being an individual*ist*, a derivation which possesses ambiguous if not negative connotations.

It is impossible to discuss the moral importance of the idea of an individual without looking at one or two of its neighbours. When we speak of ourselves as '**persons**', the idea is contentless. A child becomes a person without our saying what it has to like. A person is largely a repository of **rights** and duties ('Treat me as a person!'). A 'self' on the other hand is our inner creature. We speak of our self as tender, as needing protection, as something unfolding of its own given nature. Small children unmistakably have selves, and it is natural to associate metaphors of flowering and nurture with their **development**.

They grow up into individuals. The teacher's task is commonly agreed to be one of the shaping spirits which will make the child an individual with his or her strong 'character' (another term to be understood alongside 'person' and 'self'), preferably without unpleasant character*istics* but always with a **liberal** tolerance of the rights of persons to become whatever they freely choose to become.

The trouble with this version of an individual's **education** is that there is bad faith somewhere in it. The teacher is taught to make children *self-possessed* individuals, each to become his or her own person, to develop a strong character, to become an exciting, intelligent, feelingful individual. But **liberalism** forbids the teacher to say exactly what kind of individual the pupil should become. If the individual chooses to become like one of the characters in *Goodfellas*, a drug-trading killer, say, then the liberal teacher may regret it but cannot, in consistency, prohibit it.

Individual*ism* is, therefore, a deep difficulty and, although open to plain moral **criticism**, impossible in our kind of **society** to wave away. It is, moreover, so obviously and horribly at odds with the way of the world. Over here, in the rich countries, education makes for animated, fulfilled and self-expressive individuals; over there, in the poor ones, commanding such individualism is a cruel stupidity. Inasmuch as the moral **principles** of **liberal** individualism teach the necessities of material well-being and mutual respect as the foundation of its practice, it is damnably hard to work out how to reconcile such ideals with one's duties to others, especially those living in misery. As Marx put it, 'The condition of the free development of each is the free development of all'.

FURTHER READING

John Dunn (1979), *Western Political Theory in the Face of the Future*. Cambridge: Cambridge University Press.
Steven Lukes (1973), *Individualism*. Oxford: Oxford University Press.
Charles Taylor (1989), *Sources of the Self*. Cambridge, MA: Harvard University Press.

individual

It was during the 1840s that a newly-reforming government in Britain tackled the acute problems of conditions in the factories by appointing special inspectors to report on how factory owners met new stipulations for health and safety. At the same time, and as **society** moved towards a national system of compulsory education (not finalised until 1870), Her Majesty's Inspectors of **Schools** (HMI) were dispatched to ensure that the 'elementary schools' came up to the **standards** warranting the continuation of their state grants. The most famous of the inspectors at this time was Matthew Arnold, appointed in 1851.

Thereafter, HMI became a powerful and respected presence in the making of **education** policy until in 1993 the then Tory government dissolved HMI into a system of competing corporations, a change plaintively greeted by the Queen by asking the Secretary of State, 'I thought these people were important; what have they done wrong?'

HMI were absorbed into the Office for Standards in Education (Ofsted), which sounds like something out of *Nineteen Eighty-Four* and which started inspecting schools in 1993. HMI trained a large number of people who were then qualified to carry out the new-style inspections. To begin with, most of the people trained were existing inspectors and advisers from local education **authorities** around the country. They were trained as **subject** specialists who were team members, and some were trained as 'registered inspectors' in order to lead inspection teams.

For a primary school, the size of the team was determined by the size of the school, and subjects were shared depending on the inspectors' specialisms. For a secondary school, on the whole, the team consisted of a specialist for each subject. The team for both primary and secondary schools had to include a 'lay inspector', who did not have an educational background but had been trained, usually to inspect the more pastoral features of a school. The team, and the final report, were managed by the registered inspector.

The word 'Ofsted' became a verb, and teachers referred to being 'Ofstedded'. To begin with, schools had months of notice before an inspection, so there was plenty of time to paint the corridors and produce the necessary documentation. Then the inspectors would descend, staying, in the case of secondary schools, for a week. Both the anticipation, and the inspection itself, reduced many teachers to a fragile state. As the week went on, the registered inspector would agree the **judgements** with his or her team, and produce a lengthy report, which could be up to 100 pages long.

In 2005, the whole process was streamlined. This was not just to save money, although it certainly does that. The argument was that schools had become used to the inspection process, and now understood the judgement criteria thoroughly themselves. This meant senior leaders could organise a rigorous self-evaluation process in school ('rigour' is a favourite Ofsted word). The current inspection process uses the school's self-evaluation form (SEF) as its starting point. Inspections last for two days (for some schools, only one), and teams range in size from one inspector to four or five, depending on the size of the school. There no longer has to be a lay inspector. Reports are now only a few pages long, and go back to the school within a week after the inspection.

The scale of judgements has changed over the years, from a five-point scale, to a seven-point scale, and now four points: 1 – outstanding; 2 – good; 3 – satisfactory; 4 – inadequate (or as Ted Wragg put it, fab, brill, OK and crap). This scale is used for all judgements, for example, on lesson observations, and on all aspects in the report, which comprise: overall effectiveness of the school; **achievement** and standards, personal **development** and well-being; **teaching** and **learning**; **curriculum** and other activities; care, guidance and support; **leadership** and **management**. If a school is judged inadequate overall, it will be put in a category – either 'notice to improve' or 'special measures'. Schools in this situation will be subject to frequent monitoring visits until they are deemed to have improved enough to be 'satisfactory'. Other schools will be re-inspected after three years.

Schools now have only three days' notice of an inspection. The new, shorter inspections seem to be received better than the old ones, and inspectors say that the inspection is being carried out with the school, rather than 'done to it'.

inspection

FURTHER READING

Office for Standards in Education: www.ofsted.gov.uk

Intelligence

If **education** is the **training** of thought and **thinking**, intelligence is the word used to cover speed, facility, responsiveness, perseverance and readiness in thought. It is what teachers are most grateful for, when they encounter it, what they must comment on favourably in their reports, and yet it resists definition and nobody is quite certain what it is and whether it may be taught. For a century or more, psychologists have sought to refine intelligence tests which will yield accurate and prescriptive results, but many still fall back on the old bromide, 'intelligence is what the tests test'. Yet after the 1944 Education Act a generation of 11-year-olds in Britain had their educational futures decided by the administration of intelligence tests, and were assigned to grammar or secondary modern **schools** according to their scores and the local availability of places.

Intelligence, like all our **concepts**, is defined by its many uses in practice, each one of which is supposed to have an acknowledged referent. So to be intelligent is above all to be quick on the uptake, to be prompt and resourceful in dealing with surprises or accidents, or to be original and relevant in sorting among one's memories for occasions and **experiences** useful in addressing novel difficulties; or it is to be concentrated and attentive in pursuing solutions, imaginative and creative in the construction of patterns, relations or **ideas**. The varieties of intelligence, as Howard Gardner proposes, take several forms, and the list of intellectual **qualities** adduced here is no more than a beginning in exploration of the matter. Gardner's eight types largely derive from a taxonomy of human attributes – spatial, numerical, linguistic, emotional intelligence and so forth – but he is most concerned to break up the view that mere celerity of a testable and more or less cognitive kind is the sort of intelligence most to be prized. It will be very rare, moreover, to find human beings equipped with all forms of intelligence, and in any case it remains obscure just how much intelligence is innate and how much is learned (this is the substance of the so-called 'nature versus nurture' debate). Certainly, it is always worth keeping in mind the novelist Saul Bellow's category, 'the high IQ moron'. Everybody knows an example of a very clever person who is utterly maladroit in practical matters or completely obtuse in dealing with other people.

Teachers can be certain, however, that a child who is left unstimulated by his or her environment, who lacks active linguistic exchanges, who is not taught to know how ... and that ..., will not develop intelligently. The Russian psychologist, Vygotsky, applied himself to study the 'gap' between what a child can do alone and what can be achieved when the child is taught. Jean Piaget, his predecessor psychologist, had taught that certain kinds of **understanding** are only feasible when a child reaches a certain age; Vygotsky, agreeing with this, nonetheless showed how intrinsic the *social* **development** of **language** was to the development of intelligence. Indeed, his view was that to be intelligent was to become capable of several different kinds of speech, one modality of speech for self-regulation, another for the control of others, a third rational and social, a fourth internal (an important moment in the development of intelligence is when a child's audible monologues become silent and internal).

Cybernetics, or information **theory**, made signal differences after about 1950 to the mapping of intelligence. For our purposes, it settled something of the limitations on human intelligence, as well as the ways in which, as Bruner put it in a famous paper, children learn to go 'beyond the information given'. On the one hand, we are all limited by the number of channels of information we can process (and the more of those there are, the more intelligent one is); on the other hand, some **cultures** more than others conduce to the invention of new codes and practices.

FURTHER READING

J. S. Bruner (1913), *Beyond the Information Given*, edited by J. M. Anglin. New York: W.W. Norton.

Howard Gardner (1983), *Frames of Mind: The Theory of Multiple Intelligences*. London: Routledge.

Steven Pinker (2007), *The Stuff of Thought: Language as a Window into Human Nature*. New York: Viking.

L. S. Vygotsky (1962 [1935]), *Thought and Language*. New York: Wiley.

Gordon Wells (1981), *Learning Through Interaction: The Study of Language Development*. Cambridge: Cambridge University Press.

Nothing makes a teacher more desperate than the realisation that the **class** is 'not interested', and bringing the **attention** of a whole, more or less recalcitrant group of pupils to bear on what should be interesting is both the heaven (when you succeed) and the hell (when you don't) of being a teacher.

Plain as interest is when you see it, it is nonetheless very hard to say what constitutes it. For a start, we have to set on one side the economic meaning of the word, as denoting the charge made on a monetary loan by a bank. All the same, it turns out to be important for a teacher to explain this aspect of the **concept**, since it transpired in 2006 from a social survey of debtors holding credit cards that a substantial minority of teenagers believed that the higher the interest rate (APR) charged by a card, the better for the borrower.

Interest ranges unmanageably wide. It takes in one's legal **right** or claim upon, for instance, a dead person's estate (as left in a will); it includes the vaguer sense of one's deriving some kind of advantage from a circumstance ('I have an interest in this affair'). It begins to tighten on the **individual** when preceded by 'self', as in 'self-interest', which straightforwardly enough indicates one's response to a direct benefit to oneself from some social exchange. This in turn gives rise to the invention in economics of that key item in its algebra, 'rational self-interest', which takes for granted that the economic player in any transaction will always seek to maximise profit as a function of 'rational self-interest' and that this cipher may be used to predict **choice** and explain **behaviour**.

There is yet another sense which denotes influence or social **power**, as when one speaks of a **person**'s having an interest in the appointment of a favoured candidate for a job. Finally, however, the predominant meaning, and the one commonly used by teachers, sorts quickly among this bundle of associated meanings for interest as signifying something of importance ('this subject is of the greatest interest') *and* for the passion that **subject** may arouse ('I am most interested in this').

This last and, for readers of this book, surely most relevant sense of the word has, as you might say, its special interest as combining a quality intrinsic to the subject together with the feeling ('interestingness') it engenders. This makes the concept a happy instance of the embeddedness of **values** in facts, for the thing-in-itself possesses interest as well as the individual's being quick with an interested response.

The teacher will always have this dual meaning of interest at the back of his or her mind; will, in other words, always be commanding the topic in hand as of general *human* interest, and this is its ultimate educational justification. **Knowledge** is the product of human interests; there are matters in which pupils *ought* to be interested, and if they aren't, it is in the teacher's interest to make them so, if humanly possible. But **freedom** is socially rooted and easily learned; the teacher's duty to make life as interesting as possible is the same thing as giving it meaning. Becoming interested is then not only a feeling, but an activity and a source of meaning.

FURTHER READING

Jurgen Habermas (1972), *Knowledge and Human Interests*. London: Heinemann Educational.

David Holbrook (1965), *The Secret Places*. Cambridge: Cambridge University Press.

D. H. Lawrence (1960), *Fantasia of the Unconscious*. New York: Viking.

Martha Nussbaum (1990), *Love's Knowledge*. Oxford: Oxford University Press.

Michael Polanyi (1962), *Tacit Knowledge*. London: Routledge and Kegan Paul.

interest

Judgement

We make them all the time, but one cannot separate the word from something stern, detached, punitive, forever associated with an image of the judge in a courtroom, separated from the ordinary world by wig and gown and a position behind the bench and above the audience.

Yet a judgement is hardly different from an inference, as when we infer from the evidence of our senses that something is the case, and go ahead to act on it. Judgements are present in every reflective action, whether judgements as to immediate action ('What shall I do now?'), judgements as to future plans ('Is this a good job to go for?' 'Have I enough food in the house to feed us tonight?'), judgements of **value** ('Is this book really worth reading?'), which latter are strongly inflected by one's taste.

As we constantly notice in conversation, the same judgements may be made in different words, and it is a commonplace that our judgements vary according to our personal dispositions. Indeed, judgement is itself dispositional, as is borne out by our being able to say plausibly of somebody that 'they lack judgement', which we may put down to all sorts of such peculiarities in their disposition as their impulsiveness, lack of self-**knowledge**, partisanship or prejudice.

'Prejudice' indeed is central to **thinking** about how it is one comes to a judgement. For a prejudice comes carrying strongly disapproving overtones, but no one can make a judgement without resting it on pre-judgements, or presuppositions, about the nature of the world. The Victorian philosopher, F. H. Bradley, wrote that 'There is no such thing as a history without prejudication', and that the main thing is to be someone 'who consciously orders and creates from the known foundation of that which for him is the **truth**'.

Even this **principle** however doesn't get us past those presuppositions (or prejudices) of which a more recent philosopher, Wittgenstein, said, 'They are part of my frame of reference. If I had to give those up, I shouldn't be able to judge *anything*.'

These are momentous matters, and the differences between judgement, prejudice and presupposition are endlessly worth debating. The conditions of modern life, with – for good or evil – all its strong individualism make it more and more urgent to pass judgement on it, but these conditions are exactly those which make it less and less possible accurately to do so.

Judgements are made in school **inspections** using the 'inspection framework'. However, like any system of grading, decisions are rarely clear-cut, and inspection teams can deliberate for hours. Like most forms of **examination**, the system is not standardised, and it is possible that one team can reach a slightly different judgement from that which another team might have made.

FURTHER READING

R. G. Collingwood (1939), *An Autobiography*. Oxford: Oxford University Press.
F. R. Leavis (1975), 'Judgement and analysis', in *The Living Principle*. London: Chatto and Windus.
Christopher Ricks (1988), *T. S. Eliot and Prejudice*. London: Faber and Faber.

judgement

Justice, Plato said, is the prime **value** of a polity (a fully political **society** with an official government and tabulated laws). At its heart, justice signifies the **principle** of the distribution of rewards and **responsibilities**, of the goods as well as the more unwelcome labours necessary for **society** to thrive. The principle of justice, that is, arbitrates the three main constituents of politics – wealth, privilege and **power** – according to what a given society concludes is fair in such distribution, and 'fairness' is commonly held to be almost a synonym for justice as well as to be heard invoked as a regulative and understood appeal in everyday life in the school playground.

At the formal end of the **concept** there stands justice as the administration of law, and this sense of the concept includes those acts of punishment and 'correction' which a society or an institution visits upon those who deserve retribution. Such punishment – fines, detention, **community** service, being 'bound over', 'on probation' or watched carefully – are, in the important verb derived from the concept, 'justified' by law taking its stand upon what is necessary but not excessive for the maintenance of social order. The 'corrective' aspect of law operates, for instance, to put right some perhaps unintended but terrible accident – as when Distillers Ltd had to pay large compensation to those crippled by Thalidomide. The system of taxation with the rich paying more than the poor is a partially corrective aspect of the law, one much invoked when it seems that the payment of colossal bonuses to city bankers violates the idea of 'fairness'.

This latter case is generally argued over with regard to the force of **equality** which, since it arrived with a bang in the middle of the French and American revolutions of 1789 and 1776, has been intrinsic to the argument about justice. Justice dictates that persons may only be treated unequally because of relevant differences which need so far as possible to be put right. The various special provisions made for the disabled are examples of this. The rightly celebrated **work** of John Rawls is taken to be the best expression of modern **theories** of **liberal** justice, in which he enunciates two founding **principles**: the first, that each **person** has an equal **right** to the most extensive basic liberty compatible with a similar liberty for all others; the second, that any inequalities work in such an arrangement so that they are to everyone's advantage and attached to official positions open to all. All benefits so allocated should be such, Rawls insists, as would be agreed upon by all if they did not know in advance what social advantages (such as wealth, health, status or birth) they would have in society.

Thus, a person not knowing beforehand how rich they were, nor how strong nor intelligent nor powerful, would naturally agree on an equivalence of treatment and distribution which seemed safest, and, therefore, just. Other accounts of justice, especially the **tradition** of socialism, have preferred as rational a simpler requirement that each person gives to society according to his or her ability (products, money, talent) and takes from society according to his or her need (health, impoverishment, accident). Michael Walzer's fine book, *Spheres of Justice*, makes justice not only the key principle in every aspect of life (home, school, shops, streets, parliaments) but also relative to radical historical changefulness. He reviews a long list of worldwide examples, from the Chinese **examination** system for its civil servants which lasted 1300 years to the offices of the Puritan Commonwealth in mid-seventeenth century England, and concludes that however various justice is, it is always the opposite of tyranny. The just society must be sure to place justice under the active protection of its citizens. A just **school** is to be found in the hands of its teachers, respected as such by its pupils.

FURTHER READING

Brian Barry (1989), *Theories of Justice*. London: Harvester.
John Rawls (1971), *A Theory of Justice*. Cambridge, MA: Harvard University Press.
Michael Walzer (1983), *Spheres of Justice*. Oxford: Blackwell.

justice

The first parental answer given to the child's **question**, 'Why should I go to **school**?', is to say 'To acquire knowledge', although there is much to say after that. In any case, the child might then ask 'What's knowledge?' and the answer would be dauntingly abstract.

It might sensibly start by separating knowledge from belief by way of showing that when you know something, that something must be true, whereas when you only believe it, it may not be true. But that sense of 'knowing' leads to so many different places that all one can conclude is that there are many forms and varieties of knowledge, such that one cannot really say that knowledge, which must be true, is compounded of an aggregation of facts, for the bits and pieces of knowledge a **person** may acquire only make sense (and are therefore knowable) when placed on the right spot on the map of knowledge. Our little piece of knowledge only becomes knowable in relation to the roads and landmarks of the knowledge we already have. Watch a baby intently trying to sort out things within its reach or field of vision and you can see this map-making at a very early stage.

Even without the words, the baby begins to sort the world into things it knows ('knowing that …') and things it can do ('knowing how …'). In addition, there is that kind of knowing which is neither knowing that … nor knowing how … but is formally referred to as 'knowledge by acquaintance' and takes in the vast realm of everyday knowledge of living, from performing such natural fundamentals as breathing or eating (you don't learn how to breathe or eat, you just do these actions) to interpreting or imagining in all sorts of subtle ways how the world is and how it might be otherwise (you don't know that a piece of music will move you to tears, but it does).

Already we have some ready-to-wear distinctions in the **theory** of knowledge, but no answer to the question 'What is knowledge?' Is it something made? (To be knowledge, we already know that it can't be made up.) What is it made of (that is, does it have a form)? At first sight, we might say that it is made in a verbal (or, as in maths, a symbolic) statement, and further say that the statement must be meaningful and true. Now, a statement may meet both conditions but not be knowledge because it is unverified, or just a guess. So we have to check with the person who made the statement, and then to check on the reasons there are for believing it. Knowledge, it transpires, rests on both **authority** and evidence. Hence, at both ends – the person who knows or states, and the person who wants to know – there can be no separation between the knower and the known. It is this which leads one philosopher to say that if knowledge is indeed a kind of artefact, it is not so much like a manu-factured and replicable product (teapot or television) as it is like a **work of art**. It has been made by the knower in response to questions put to his or her experience and history. It is a product of reflection on **experience**, verbal or symbolic knowledge-making being like an effort to produce a perfect reflection in a mirror of the original object while every effort to make the reflection exactly right is then copied from the mirror in *another* mirror.

Some people have concluded that this is actually how science works, which is to say it moves further and further back from the original facts of experience until it has turned its components into such very general abstractions that only then may they be in turn transformed into for-mulae and general laws. Einstein's famous equation $e = mc^2$, where e is energy, m is mass and c the speed of light or 180,000 miles per second, offers to hold at poise all the phenomena of space and time, of matter and motion. But it is an expression, made, shaped, compressed and sim-plified, a very long way from the bombarding particles and swooping waves which compose our bodies and the heavens.

That natural science has achieved its successes by the use of what have been called 'experience-distant' **concepts** gives rise to the device of the so-called 'scale of forms of knowledge'. On this scale, religion comes historically first, as the earliest and longest-lived attempt to make a system out of inquiry and to turn inquiry into knowledge; art comes sec-ond, deploying the basic human gift for storytelling and as being the effort to organise the faculty of **imagination** thereby to make it produce myths for living reasonably. On some scales, science is third, as being the labour to transcribe the facts of the natural world into classifications and laws, and history and philosophy finish as queens of the forms because concerned with the human and *changeful* nature of knowledge, and the past – that different country – as providing the only source of self-knowledge from which to build the future.

On other scales, however, science is queen because it is triumphantly capable of certainty. For our part, we doubt this. Science is cocksure but itself a historical product and properly to be understood historically. Science has taught humanity arrogance as well as bringing (for some) longevity; the danger the globe is now in suggests that the cautions of history are timely.

FURTHER READING

Marjorie Grene (1966), *The Knower and the Known*. London: Faber and Faber.
David Pears (1971), *What is Knowledge?* London: Allen and Unwin.
Bertrand Russell (1948), *Human Knowledge: Its Scope and Limits*. London: Allen and Unwin.

Language

The word 'language' derives from the word for 'tongue'. This is understandable, as the sounds required for language are made by different positions of the tongue. The **principle** of language depends on a particular sound or group of sounds representing a specific object (or **person**, place, action, feeling and so on). A linguist would refer to the signifier (usually a word, but there is also sign language), and the signified (what the word represents). The term 'language' refers to the overall **concept** and also to individual languages (which are sometimes called 'tongues').

Language is an astonishing phenomenon and is the **subject** of massive study and research. It is thought that a language system, with distinct and distinguishable sounds, developed over 100,000 years ago (this has been deduced from fossils of the vocal tract, which needed to evolve in order to produce differentiated vowel sounds).

Many of the languages of Europe and India have similar features, and it is believed that they evolved from a single language. This parent language was designated Proto-Indo-European. As groups of speakers migrated across Asia and Europe, their language continued to change. Their **communities** were completely out of contact with others, so it is easy to see how different languages developed. Later, of course, tribes started to move again, attack and invade, so languages clashed, and then influenced each other.

Individual words were grouped together in different ways, as systems of grammar emerged. Subtle changes developed to denote tense, or number, or relationships between people and their actions (or their belongings). Once writing developed, the **structure** of grammar in a particular language became more fixed.

Language became political. The ruling group used their own language for government. Subordinate groups clung to their language as a symbol of their **identity**, but this isolated them from the centre of power. Nowadays, nationalist groups are anxious to prevent their language dying out. However, English, in one of its forms (usually 'American English'), is becoming more and more a global language for matters of business, trade and negotiation.

As the main medium of **communication** between human beings (together with 'body language'), spoken language is obviously crucial to children's emotional and intellectual **development**. Most children pick it up surprisingly easily, considering its complexity, although it is not easy for those with particular **learning** difficulties or disabilities. Children need to be exposed to language as early as possible, when the brain is most receptive to it. Interaction with others is crucial, so children in their early years will not develop language through being plonked in front of a television.

Children not only acquire language – they learn to vary it, and use forms with different nuances (or 'registers'). They quickly find out that you do not talk to your teacher, or your granny, in the same way that you speak to your friends or your little brother. Later on, they will probably use inappropriate language deliberately. In some families, children are bilingual, and can readily switch from one language to another. In **schools**, some pupils arrive speaking little English, and it is vital that they catch up as quickly as possible.

Improving all pupils' language **skills** is a crucial aspect of **work** in school. This has to happen in all parts of the **curriculum**, not just in '**literacy**' or English. Pupils have to become more and more aware of how language is used in different contexts. Many pupils will use their own registers or dialects in various social situations. However, a school has a **responsibility** to ensure pupils have a command of the dominant form of English in this country, '**standard** English'. In a multicultural society a rich variety of idioms will enter the classroom, and these should be appreciated. But it is just as necessary to teach these children the forms of standard English. Not to do so is to deprive children of the dominant form of a national language, which they need in order to play a full part in social and political life.

Language is not just used in a business-like way, but also for fun and entertainment, as in jokes, puns, riddles, crosswords and other games, and also in literature. A single word can be seen as a metaphor – a sound representing something else; in poetry, metaphor carries representation to new levels.

FURTHER READING

C. Brumfit (1995), *Language Education in the National Curriculum.* Oxford: Blackwell.

Pater Burke and Roy Porter (1987), *The Social History of Language.* Cambridge: Cambridge University Press.

David Crystal (1995), *The Cambridge Encyclopaedia of the English Language.* Cambridge: Cambridge University Press.

N. Mercer and J. Swann (1996), *Learning English: Development and Diversity.* Oxford: Oxford University Press.

'Lazy' carries almost equal approbatory and disapproving charges. 'Lazy days in summer', 'lazing by the beach' only need the adjective for a wistful dreaminess to come over one's **imagination**. But to accuse a pupil of being lazy or to adduce 'laziness' on a school report is to reach for one of the teacher's most severe and final sentences of condemnation.

Yet the **quality** itself is opaque, and loose in application. No doubt some people have a turn in their temperament towards indolence; they are not highly energised in any particular direction; their manner, often amiable and indiscriminate, is sleepy, perhaps good-humoured, rarely malign. These are, no doubt, dispositionally lazy people and there's nothing much to be done about it. (Sometimes a whole **culture** may be described as lazy, generally associated with tropical islands and natural plenty.)

'Laziness' used as a term of teacherly abuse, however, is about as precise as 'boring' when used as a term of pupil abuse and directed at a lesson. It means little more than that the pupil betrays regular inattention and the keen **question** is then what it is that truly holds the lively attentiveness of which every growing creature is composed and which is so needful to the process of growth itself. The opposite of lazy is not so much 'energetic' as it is 'thoughtful' or 'concentrated'.

Laziness itself gets such a bad name from the Puritan **tradition** which, from about 1600, taught that **work** redeemed the vices of sloth and gluttony and the rest, even though only faith could save a soul. To be lazy, therefore, was to be damned, and this version of Martin Luther's sixteenth-century Christianity became gradually secularised until teachers inherited the unquestioned antinomy, hardworking versus lazy, and 'lazy' carried along with it awful connotations of self-indulgence and a lax refusal to use one's proper talents to the full and to realise one's **potential**.

It is doubtless one of the teacher's duties to put down habitual laziness and to teach the lessons of our civilisation that a pupil shall learn the **discipline** of routinised work. It is one aspect of **wisdom**, however, to know that laziness is from time to time restorative, that it is in a state of lazing around that one may receive some of one's best and most unexpected insights, that the occasional refusal of discipline and labour is a proper sign of **freedom**. The Romantic poet, John Keats, commended a state of mind he called 'Negative Capability', 'when a man is capable of being in uncertainties, Mysteries, doubts, without any irritable reaching after fact and reason'. This is the best aspect of laziness.

FURTHER READING

Desiderius Erasmus, *In Praise of Folly* (1500).
Kenneth Grahame (1906), *The Wind in the Willows*. London: Methuen.
John Keats (1954), *Selected Letters*, edited by F. Page. Oxford: World's Classics.

key concepts in education

Leadership

Leaders have to be able to inspire and motivate others. They have to have a vision of where they're going that others can accept. This vision may extend well into the future, so **individuals** have to be convinced that their actions now will enable future generations to reap the benefit. For religious leaders, the vision may reach into the afterlife, and their followers are inspired by a description of heaven. Leaders in time of war have to inspire soldiers through patriotism, and make them believe that, if they die, it is in a good cause.

> Once more unto the breach, dear friends, once more;
> Or close the wall up with our English dead!' (*Henry V*, Act 3, Scene 1)

The key to this kind of leadership is oratory, which will evoke energy and passion in others to do what the leader says. A real example is Winston Churchill's speech on 4 June 1940 which, in Simon Schama's words, 'turned the tide'.

It does not always follow, however, that the leader with fine oratory actually knows what he or she is talking about. Sometimes, people are persuaded into an action that is a complete folly – to fight a particular battle, perhaps, or to invest their money in something that turns out to be worthless, or, in the case of some religious cults, to commit suicide. It is worth reflecting that 'leader' translates as *führer* in German and *duce* in Italian, the titles adopted by Hitler and Mussolini.

Where the audience is more pragmatic, people like to feel that their leader has credibility, and is making decisions from practical **knowledge** based on **experience**. This would apply to someone such as a sports captain, and would certainly apply to a headteacher. There has to be vision, but it must be well grounded in practicality. Headteachers have to sustain a collective vision for the school, and also maintain a positive organisational **culture** and climate. This involves putting policies in place, and then making sure they are followed. The headteacher cannot do this on his or her own, and this has resulted in the **development** of 'distributed leadership', which requires delegation and shared **responsibility**. It is not surprising that schools now speak of their 'leadership teams'. This is a more consultative, democratic model than that of the one autocratic, if inspiring, leader. It is the model promoted by the National College of School Leadership, which offers training and qualifications such as 'National Professional Qualification for Headship' and 'Leading from the Middle'.

However, as in any hierarchical organisation, one leader takes more responsibility than others, and is seen to be the most accountable. In a crisis (for example, when a school goes into special measures), a leader is needed who can draw on all of his or her charisma, and lead the staff out of the mire. Sometimes, you also need luck, as football managers would agree.

FURTHER READING

Mark Brundrett, Neil Smith and Robert Smith (eds) (2003), *Leadership in Education*. London: Sage.

Brent Davies (ed.) (2005), *The Essentials of School Leadership*. London: Paul Chapman.

Brent Davies and Tim Brighouse (eds) (2008), *Passionate Leadership in Education*. London: Sage.

John MacBeath, John M. Gray, Jane Cullan, David Frost, Susan Steward, Sue Swaffield (eds) (2006), *Schools on the Edge: Responding to Challenging Circumstances*. London: Paul Chapman.

Graham Haydon (2007), *Values for Educational Leadership*. London: Sage.

C. D. C. Reeve (1989), *Philosopher Kings*. Princeton: Princeton University Press.

National College for School Leadership: www.ncsl.org.uk

Learning

The verb 'to learn' has kept the same meaning from Old English: to acquire **knowledge**; to receive information. Of these, 'to receive information' sounds a very passive function, similar to the role of the pupils in *Hard Times*, who were 'little pitchers ... to be filled so full of facts'.

In classrooms nowadays learning should be active, and lessons are judged on how pupils are engaged in their learning, and how well they participate. Passivity is out. Teachers are required to set up activities so that pupils can investigate for themselves, work in groups, or share **ideas** in pairs. Other **strategies** include peer **teaching**, and peer evaluation. Pupils should reflect on their learning at the end of the lesson. This can be grandly called 'metacognition' – thinking about their own thought processes.

Teachers are also meant to have a knowledge of pupils' 'learning styles'. These can be auditory – some pupils like to sit and listen; visual – these pupils take in visual images and demonstrations; and kinaesthetic, which sounds like the pupils who can't sit still. In fact, 'kinaesthetic' signifies 'learning by doing', which is generally acknowledged to be the best way of learning anyway.

This distinction between pupils' learning styles is artificial, as all three styles are needed for different purposes. Pupils can't start 'learning by doing' until they have been told what to do and why (auditory), and seen an example (visual). It is important that the styles are combined, rather than being considered as exclusive.

'Personalised learning' refers to the tailoring of the **curriculum** to **individual** needs and aspirations. Pupils are also encouraged to undertake 'independent learning', by carrying out research on their own, without the intervention of a teacher. Certainly teachers are not necessary for learning to take place, and nor even are books or computers. We can learn from a new sight, sound or **experience**.

Pupils are now often referred to as 'learners', to emphasise the active nature of the process, and the part they play. We are all learners: lifelong learning is the aim.

learning

FURTHER READING

Jerome Bruner (1971), *The Relevance of Education*. New York: W. W. Norton.

Margaret Donaldson (1978), *Children's Minds*. London: Fontana.

Debra McGregor (2007), *Developing Thinking: Developing Learning*. Maidenhead: Open University Press.

David Wood (1988), *How Children Think and Learn*. Oxford: Blackwell.

Liberal

The origins of the word are, of course, found in the name of 'liberty', or **freedom** herself. The adjective 'liberal' comes first to be used in the seventeenth century as referring to a particular class of free men, bound by none of the laws or conventions of a then disintegrating feudalism, and thereafter (by 1700 or so) the word collected its more modern associations with both open-handedness ('liberal with one's gifts') and with freedom of thought, creativity and speculation (supplying the title among the **disciplines** of **learning** of 'the liberal **arts**').

During the period of the Enlightenment in the second half of the eighteenth century, when philosophical innovation and political upheaval went hand-in-hand, 'liberal' began to gather to itself associations of moral, political and religious free-**thinking** – which meant unorthodox, heretical, subversive and so forth. The liberal became a figure for whom the powers of reason replaced the **authority** of **tradition**, and to whom the rational **methods** of science were a better guide for **society** than the sovereignty of a ruling **class**.

By the end of the eighteenth century these same attitudes of **mind** were called to the service of Romanticism in the arts, and the complexities of modern liberalism began to take shape: on one side, the liberal followers of the philosopher Jeremy Bentham, who put their trust in the science of politics guided by a careful, monumental accumulation of social facts; on the other, liberalism was associated with the rejection of social convention and the radical individuation of such Romantic artists as Byron, Shelley, Beethoven and Turner.

Either way, liberal thought and expression were progressive, even revolutionary, and when a political party took the name 'Liberal' to itself, it commanded support through the nineteenth century from all those who wanted to move **society** towards greater **equality** and individual freedom – whether for the poor, for children, or for women.

Liberalism gradually accrued a dual and contradictory meaning. The hard liberal professes the freedom of the **individual** as paramount (this became particularly associated in the twentieth century with economic liberalism, or the freedom for capital to do as it likes). The soft liberal defends individual freedom only insofar as it does not constrain the

liberal

freedom of others: when my freedom of action jars on yours, then mine must be curtailed in order to permit yours commensurate room to move.

Socialism as a political doctrine emerged from the thought of such radical writers as Karl Marx and William Morris after the European revolutions of 1848 as an effort to show how to bring a truly liberal society to birth, one in which 'the free **development** of each depends on the free development of all'.

This last formula has been deeply influential in guiding educational reform during the second half of the twentieth century and beyond. Liberalism may still be said, in its various forms, to be the political and pedagogical victor of the titanic clash of theorists of society which produced two world wars and one cold one. It is now struggling to keep faith with its keystone **principle** of freedom, while acknowledging the forceful demands of those principles which clash with freedom – notably equality, social justice and, nameless but unignorable, the turning of the globe itself, its atmosphere, its plenty and its natural health – against the habit of free exploitation which liberal economics has taken for granted.

FURTHER READING

Richard Bellamy (1994), *In Defence of Liberalism*. Cambridge: Cambridge University Press.
John Dunn (1979), *Western Political Theory in the Face of the Future*. Cambridge: Cambridge University Press.
John Stuart Mill (1991 [1874]), *On Liberty and Other Essays*. Oxford: Oxford University Press.

Literacy

Most children learn to talk fairly easily. In contrast, **learning** to read and write is a laborious process. It is the ability to read and write which makes a person 'literate', with varying degrees of fluency.

The first 200 years after the introduction of the printing press saw a rapid growth in literacy, so that around a third of men in England (but fewer women) could read and write to some extent. There was then a huge increase in the nineteenth century, and by 1900 the majority of the population was literate. There were still a few pockets of illiteracy, mainly in large cities.

Arguments were already raging about **methods** of **teaching** reading, and whether children's **understanding** was good enough. In 1895, one of Her Majesty's Inspectors gave his views:

> Of intelligent reading, however, there is but little, and more determined and persistent effort on the part of teachers is needed, to get children to understand what they read. It is but seldom that they are able to give a synonym for an ordinary word in their reading lesson or to express the meaning of a phrase or sentence in their own words. (Committee of Councils on Education 1845–99 Minutes and Reports, London HMSO)

These arguments continue. It has been stated that nowadays a quarter of children leave primary school unable to read. What actually happens is that over 80 per cent leave with a 'level 4' or better in English (level 4 being the 'expected' level at age 11). Of the remaining children, many have reached level 3 – so it is not true to say they cannot read; they can read, but not well enough to get level 4. There is a small number of children with specific learning difficulties who are unable to read.

How literate do people need to be? For their own safety, they need to read road signs, and instructions. 'Functional literacy' has been described as the ability to read a tax form (which is demanding, in every sense of the word). 'Higher-order' reading skills include inference, deduction and an understanding of the effect of **language**. These **skills** are necessary in everyday life in order to recognise when someone is trying to pull the wool over our eyes.

literacy

Enjoyment of reading comes beyond mere functionality. 'Reading for pleasure' usually means fiction, or 'literature' (novels and poetry which have achieved status in a **society**). People who read for pleasure are fluent readers who respond to the writer's **choice** of language. Appreciation of literature widens our **experience** and understanding of others. However, reading fiction is not a moral **virtue** in itself. Many people prefer to read non-fiction.

Similarly, there is a basic level of writing which is necessary in order to function in society. More advanced writers enjoy crafting the language, whether they are writing a report, or a story. The crucial factor is whether a piece of writing – however short – communicates clearly to the audience for whom it is intended.

In schools, children's literacy has to be good enough to cope with the demands of all **subjects**, not just English. Even practical subjects require reading, for example, understanding information, and writing, in planning and evaluation. These demands were recognised in the Bullock Report (*A Language for Life*, DES 1975) which coined the phrase 'language policy across the **curriculum**'.

The problem is that good readers and writers get better because they enjoy using their skills, and children who are weaker in literacy do not improve at the same rate, so the gap widens across the years.

In 1997, the Literacy Strategy was launched in primary schools to address some of the difficulties inherent in teaching reading and writing. This established a rigid methodology through the Literacy Hour, but it has become more flexible over the past 10 years. It now addresses speaking and listening as well as reading and writing, although strictly it is the last two that make a person 'literate'. However, it is obvious that the **development** of spoken language skills is crucial to the ability to read, write and communicate well.

Nowadays phrases such as 'IT literacy' and even 'emotional literacy' are used, which stretch the word beyond its original meaning.

FURTHER READING

Margaret Meek (1991), *On Being Literate*. Oxford and London: Bodley Head.

Elaine Millard (1997), *Differently Literate: Boys, Girls and the Schooling of Literacy.* London: Falmer Press.

The Bullock Report (1975), *A Language for Life*, London: DES.

The word 'manage' seems to have come into English from the Italian *maneggiare* which means to handle, especially to handle or train horses. This is interesting given its use in **education** relating to the management of people (both children and adults). It also means providing the over-all day-to-day administration, and this applies to **schools** as well as to businesses and other organisations.

Historically, managers were agents (for example, farm managers), rather than owners or employers. This is the case in schools, where the local **authority**, or the governors, would be the employers. In industry, at different times, the interests of 'management' and 'workers' have often been in conflict, and then usually resolved by compromise, unless one side capitulates.

The word 'management' came to be used widely in schools during the 1980s. Before that, the headmaster or headmistress (before the time that they all became 'headteachers') and the deputy heads had specific roles, but were not yet called 'the senior management team'. Once this term was used, other layers followed – line managers, middle managers. This meant that staffing within a school had a clear **structure**, with lines of **responsibility**. Gone were the days when, for example, a **subject** department in a secondary school would operate fairly autonomously.

Also during the 1980s, schools had to adopt the conventions of action planning and produce a 'school management plan', usually a three-year plan. This coincided with 'local management of schools' which meant that **individual** schools took charge of their own budgets, rather than these being controlled by the local authority.

In schools, all teachers are managers insofar as they manage their own classrooms, and manage groups of pupils ('**behaviour** management'). It has been suggested that experienced managers from the world of business could be brought in to run schools. However, they would lack the **experience** of working with children. A headteacher who has been a successful classroom practitioner has credibility with his or her staff, and can also establish good relationships with pupils (who can be a pretty diverse bunch).

A crucial strand of management in schools nowadays is 'performance management'. This is usually carried out by line managers on an annual basis. It is to appraise performance, and set targets for improvement. The

management

129

argument is that however good performance is, there is always room for improvement.

'**Leadership** and management' are usually put together, but they represent different qualities. A headteacher, for example, might be a good leader but not a good manager. He or she could provide the vision, but would need someone else to put it into practice. A good leader needs to motivate people and make staff feel valued, but also to have a realistic view of strengths and weaknesses. Implementation of the vision should lead to improvements. Good leaders should consult others, and take account of evidence. They shouldn't jump to conclusions, and assume that they are always right.

Thus far, the concept seems harmlessly matter-of-fact and practical. Management has, however, become over the past generation not only paramount among the policy sciences, but an ideology in its own right, offering to solve and satisfy all administrative difficulties by way of its special techniques, ordered in its own inimitable and often fatuous jargon. Thus, one of its innumerable handbooks commends to all members of the institution in question (Ofsted as it happens) the preparation of 'personal development objectives' as tested against 'corporate learning priorities'; 'competencies' are to be drawn up as 'frameworks' in the name of 'learning development' and a policy of universal 'empowerment' will shape into improbable unity the definition of an institutional 'vision'.

This is a language in which it is impossible to tell the **truth**. Management science, so-called, is a device of modern bureaucracies the purpose of which is to conceal the facts of conflict by pretending there is no such thing, and to persuade subordinates to comply with decisions plainly against their own best **interests**. The dreadful **language** of management is part of the effort to invent a technology for the elimination of dissent and disobedience, and to ensure as far as possible the superimposition of planning and routine upon all aspects of human conduct. It doesn't quite go without saying that such systems are (unconsciously or not) hostile both to the **art** of teaching, the growth of autonomy, and the discovery of one's own responsibilities.

FURTHER READING

Tony Bush and Les A. Bell (eds) (2002), *The Principles and Practice of Educational Management.* London: Sage.
Mary Douglas (1990), *Can Institutions Think?* London: Routledge.
Anthony Giddens (1997), *The Consequences of Modernity.* Cambridge: Polity Press.
Jeff Jones (2004), *Management Skills in Schools.* London: Paul Chapman.

Meritocracy

Meritocracy was the neologism coined by Michael Young as the key **concept** of what he saw as a new kind of **society** shaping itself in 1950. This concept identifies a social group rising to **power** strictly (or so it believes) on account of its own intrinsic merits, whether merits of **intelligence**, ability, charm, talent, specialised **experience**, or just the gift of getting on with other people and, as they say, 'making things happen'. The main point about the meritocrat is that his or her success ratifies the **principle** of **equality** of opportunity because in no way depending upon prior and unearned privileges of birth, inheritance, **education** or social **class**. The power and position of a meritocrat is, he or she believes, consequent only upon intrinsic merit; theirs are therefore well deserved rewards in a social race in which everybody starts equal.

There is, of course, bad faith in all this, since nobody can start on equal terms with everyone else; there are always advantages and disabilities of class, genes, **gender**, colour, money and so forth which make perfect equality of opportunity impossible to achieve and in itself undesirable in any case.

But the meritocrat has this further disagreeable attitude, that since his or her power and status have been well and fairly earned by personal talent and effort, the less fortunate also are getting their just deserts and if those deserts are meagre and unfulfilling, too bad. Widespread ruthlessness of this kind may be seen throughout contemporary society; its reverse side, no less widespread, is self-pity.

It follows from these attitudes and their attendant **ideology** that the cultural continuities of class and neighbourhood are thinned out, and history itself disregarded as the compelling force in social formation. This error is characteristic of **liberals** and their **theories** of **management**.

It must, therefore, be the concerns of **schools** to balance the just rewards of meritocratic advance (which is a fundamental of the system) against the no less powerful duties towards equality of respect, mutuality, trust and putting down arrogance and conceit.

meritocracy

FURTHER READING

Michael Young (1951), *The Rise of the Meritocracy*. Harmondsworth: Penguin.

A person who is wholly unmethodical is crazy to think at all, and cannot make those thoughts to correspond with the world. The grounding of inquiry on dependable observation or agreed-upon **truths** or reasons, without which such necessities as deduction, induction, **judgement** and verification cannot be discovered, becomes meaningless. For example, we establish the form of a given proposition by determining what its contradiction or negation would look like. In other words, it must be clear that to insert 'not' into a proposition does in truth negate it.

This sounds so obvious as to be silly. But it is the only way we can be sure of what we are saying. Something is the case or is not the case, if we are to have a proposition which will stand still enough to be considered. Like so much else in modern thought, it was Descartes in the early seventeenth century who was the first pioneer of method in science, and the influence of his *Discourse on Method* is still pervasive. Method varies according to whether one's inquiry may be called empirical (based on observation and sense-**experience**), analytic (pursued by way of the meaning of the words with which one thinks), rationalist (founded on trustfulness in reasoning), metaphysical (perhaps hardest of all, and indicating thought 'beyond the physical', which is to say the methodical consideration of the ultimate or absolute forms of being and of human presuppositions about the world and its universes).

Every **subject** or **discipline** has its special method, of which the two main competitors are science and history, each vying with the other to claim victory. Francis Bacon, at the start of the seventeenth century, was of the view that the basis of verification (which is plainly the heart of the matter for scientists) is *counting*: when you have counted enough instances to support your hypothesis, it's *probably* true, and you have, in the statisticians' phrase, 'permission to proceed'. Later scientists, led by Sir Isaac Newton, insisted that method must seek causation and that the discovery of causes yielded explanations in the form of laws.

Discussion of laws had led naturally to the problem of 'teleology', which is the belief (or the rational conclusion drawn) that natural processes tend towards a particular realisation. For Darwin, the first great non-theistic teleologist, species have sought spontaneously for a condition of ideal adaptation. Although believers in a god who has deliberately designed the world teleologically try to rebut Darwin by saying that nature is so comprehensively planned and interlocking that it *must* be intentional, they ignore the way evolution goes wrong, species disappear, as well as the very recent appearance and uncertain continuity of the humanity they believe to be the focus of creation.

Historians admonish scientists by saying that method and the **knowledge** it yields are both historically changeful, and that our methodicality depends on **concepts** and **principles** emerging from the past, always liable to dissolution or at least to instability in the present. The historian of these tendencies, Thomas Kuhn, has studied what he calls 'paradigm shifts' which are the moments when the weight of new evidence breaks down the old principles which scientists struggle to protect, and new methods are compelled upon the systems of inquiry. His contention is that modern science itself is radically historical, and the product of a specific **culture** and **structure** of belief at odds with older forms of science (for example, Chinese), and itself intelligible only to the times and places which thought it up.

However this may be, scientific method itself is overdue for **criticism**, never more so than in the so-called methodology courses required of graduate students in the social sciences in general, and **education** in particular. These give rise to and express what we might call the **ideology** of organisations whereby methodology subtends bureaucratic **authority** and ensures the subordination of others (in the case in hand, of **schools** to universities). Social science methodology, purportedly aping scientific method proper, teaches that the study of organisations has as its point the eradication of conflict and the promotion of efficiency (largely a cost-benefit quantity). Thus, institutions are defined as a congeries of interest groups (teachers, parents, **management**, pupils) to be managed for 'outcomes' (as they say) and **targets**. What is lacking is any conception of the institution (the school) as being in pursuit of a common good transcending partiality and realisable by the **individual** only as an actor in a **community** with its own acknowledged ends and goals. The common good of a school is compounded of a shared **identity** issuing in the fulfilment of such common purposes as the creation of an active citizenry, a humane culture, a courteous polity, a living **tradition**. Social science methodology cannot imagine such realities, and serves to warn teachers-as-students of the untrustworthiness and contingency of method, of the obvious truth that method is constructed out of partiality and partisanship, the limitations of its creators and the preferences of **power**.

method

133

FURTHER READING

Paul Feyerabend (1972), *Against Method*. London: Verso.

T. S. Kuhn (1962), *The Structure of Scientific Revolutions*. Chicago: University of Chicago Press.

Alasdair MacIntyre (1999), 'Social science methodology as ideology', in K. Knight (ed.), *The MacIntyre Reader*. Cambridge: Polity Press.

Karl Popper (1959), *The Logic of Scientific Discovery*. London: Routledge and Kegan Paul.

John Ziman (1973), *Reliable Knowledge*. London: Routledge and Kegan Paul.

key concepts in
education

Mind

The evolution, **development**, cultivation and instruction of the mind is the whole point of **education**, and yet it is still mysterious to us as to what the mind actually is. On the rare occasions when people reflect on the motions of the mind, the chances are they draw on the historically long-lived conclusions of René Descartes who, in the seventeenth century, dedicated himself to determining the **knowledge** of which he could be absolutely certain and, by steadily doubting everything which we take for granted in the world – **experience**, memory, history – what his senses told him (because they might be mistaken) came down to his famous and fundamental conclusion: 'I think, therefore I am'. This conclusion cannot be doubted not because it is provable – proof doesn't come into it – but because the **thinking** mind can go no further back and still be thinking. Knowledge of your own mind was, for Descartes, the most certain kind of knowledge you can have.

Then, he had to puzzle out the relation between mind and brain (he practised dissection and worked on eyes and the theory of vision). The brain receives the messages and, as we now know, transmits them by neuro-impulse to the appropriate parts of the body. But at the same time, the mind lights up and the **individual** has thoughts and feelings, makes **judgements** and decides to act all at the same time. How do the physical impulses and reactions turn into thoughts and feelings, mental images and **ideas**?

This has remained one of life's deepest puzzles, and is known as 'the mind–body problem'. Descartes, being as he was bound to be at the time a Christian (of a very unusual and theologically creative kind), resolved the puzzle by distinguishing between the mortal body and the immortal soul which, being a good physiologist, he pictured as tied together in the pineal gland at the very centre of the brain. At that glandular point, he theorised, physical messages turned into mental phenomena.

The Cartesian picture of what came to be called in the twentieth century 'the ghost in the machine' (by Gilbert Ryle) still lurks in many people's idea of the mind. Ryle's **criticism** was however pungent. He mocked the idea of the ghost in the machine because, he said, we don't understand the world by translating the thoughts of other people into thoughts of our own; we understand it in terms of what they do and say. The mind is not a place, nor a sort of agent doing what it does behind someone's features; it is a human being in action, just as the joint actions

mind

of a **society** of human beings enshrine and dramatise their ideas in a **culture**. There is no ghost, there is only significant action by other people more or less like ourselves. If we say of someone that she is a skilful pianist, that skilfulness is not a quality existing in the mind and then transferred to the hand on the keyboard, it is what happens when the piano is played.

Abandoning the ghost is not a matter of its being disproved, but of finding a more satisfactory way of discussing the mind. Over the centuries, different faculties or functionings of the mind have been discerned by the theorists of human nature, although it is vital to add that those theorists remain always convinced of the psychic unity of humankind: all normal humans are equipped with the same cognitive machinery, although as we know they develop it and use it differentially. All normal humans, that is, may so quicken their brains that their minds move from a state of mere consciousness to imagining, remembering, perceiving, reasoning (in various forms, such as reasoning logically or inductively or inferring), feeling.

It is obvious when one lists these faculties or functionings of the mind that they are not by any means wholly separate, nor is it agreed that reasoning and feeling may go together. For many centuries, reason and emotion have been thought of as inherently opposed to one another, and that moreover to be rational was to be able to suppress one's passions. Since the Romantic movement began in the late eighteenth century, emotion has been given a more central and welcoming status in the **concept** of the mind, and this newer envisioning of the mind has indicated that it is feelings which shape and inform experience; the task for the mind is then to summon up those feelings best suited to the experience one is living through. This, it hardly needs saying, is far from being a straightforward or wholly voluntary business.

Finally, although it is usual and understandable that we think of our minds as our own, and have learned how hard it is to gain access to other minds, the human mind, in spite of this, works and creates collectively, even if it does so by way of conflict and competition. The great achievements of culture are collective; our inmost mind (as we suppose it to be) is, for all its peculiarity and self-possession, the product of past minds out of whose thinking we build our own.

FURTHER READING

Simon Blackburn (1999), *Think*. Oxford: Oxford University Press.
R. G. Collingwood (1938), *The Principles of Art*. Oxford: Oxford University Press.
D. C. Dennett and Richard Hofstadter (1982), *The Mind's I*. Harmondsworth: Penguin.
Gilbert Ryle (1949), *The Concept of Mind*. Oxford: Oxford University Press.

Morality

This is surely the largest topic in this whole book and at the same time the most pressing **responsibility** the schoolteacher has. He or she will certainly be called to account for the moral **behaviour** of the pupils, and is regularly blamed in the yellow press for the general belief that 'children no longer know the difference between right and wrong'.

Whatever else morality may be, it certainly is expected to provide an account of this difference. But we carry unnoticingly around with us a huge moral vocabulary compounded of fragments of unintegrated moral **theories** often devised for forms of conduct from long-gone **societies** and each variously in irreconcilable conflict with one another. Thus, Aristotle's doctrine of the 'magnanimous man' (and his theories of ethics had nothing to say about women) is quite at odds with the Christian doctrine of humility. The 'act-utilitarian', so-called because of his (it's a manly no-nonsense creed) view that the only thing that matters is what the consequences of an action will be for the sum of human welfare, can make no sense of the emotivist, taught by the Romantic movement to do what *feels* right.

Sorting out a coherent and rational morality from this fragmentary inheritance is very difficult for any teacher, and it is no surprise that this modern condition drives some people back into exclusive doctrines of morality, often religious ones, and makes them refuse all legitimacy to any other morality. At the same time, trying to accommodate the sheer variety of ethical schemes in the world, other people subscribe to a moral relativism, according to which all moralities are equivalent and suit different peoples according to different **cultures**. So what is cannibalism over here is lunch over there.

Nonetheless most people remain pretty serious about the **question** of how to live their lives as best they can, and it is as well to begin from the historical (and sociological) truth, firmly set out by Alasdair MacIntyre, that moral systems are themselves forms of social **structure**; they arise from a particular form of life, and our present moral conflicts and contradictions are the more acute for being as much global as local affairs.

Given the difficulties, it may look reasonable to follow the available calculus of utilitarianism, first, because in a world of mass numbers it offers a way of calculating what to do by virtue of how the figures add up; second,

morality

because its single measure is human material benefit and comfort (food, shelter, health, safety) and we all want those; third, because its sums are secular and keep us out of religious dispute; fourth, because its grand **principle** of maximum human welfare makes life so much easier, as keeping us out of all those bitter arguments about what one ought to do. The trouble with this scheme – which is probably the scheme generally invoked on behalf of the human race by its largest common bodies such as the UN, the WHO or the World Bank – is that it misses out so much which people long for as the content of happiness: love, for instance, **freedom**, rejoicing, fulfilment … cost-benefit analysis is a chilly instrument, and the good teacher will hardly want to calculate moral **choices** for the pupils in such terms. What, after all, is the 'utility' of novels? or sport? or music? or pure maths?

The trouble is that utilitarianism, the only world morality there is, has nothing to say in answer to these questions, nor does it know what to do when faced by matters of, say, **individual** cruelty or injustice; the utilitarian, Bernard Williams tells us, is committed to doing 'the least bad thing'. Examples of this crop up daily in the hideous civil wars of our time where the utilitarian is committed not to best principles but to least resistance: refugee camps not mass slaughter.

The inadequacy of this is common **knowledge**, and in the less desperate circumstances of **school** it is probably best if teachers stick to the two universal moral principles which may be said to have won a kind of victory in the modern world, or have at least shown themselves plainly preferable to state brutality, religious bigotry or nationalist vengefulness. The two moral principles, **liberal** maybe but utilitarian certainly not, are, first (and originating in but independent of Christianity) do unto others as you would they should do unto you; second, make of your life a narrative (a **work** of art, one could say) of the best **person** you have it in you to become.

This latter quest, only terminable by the end of life, is commensurate, even synonymous with the beautiful **idea**, enshrined in the American Declaration of Independence of 1776, of life as the pursuit of happiness.

key concepts in education

FURTHER READING

Alasdair MacIntyre (1967), *A Short History of Ethics*. London: Routledge and Kegan Paul.
Iris Murdoch (1970), *The Sovereignty of Good*. London: Routledge and Kegan Paul.
Bernard Williams (1985), *Ethics and the Limits of Philosophy*. London: Fontana.

Multiculturalism

Any word with the suffix '-ism' announces itself as carrying ideological luggage and, however fishy this luggage may sometimes smell, no one can travel very far intellectually without it. So the arguments, beliefs, platitudes and superstitions of multiculturalism came gradually into being from the 1970s onwards, because **liberal** political **ideology** needed, for its own stability and coherence, a system of thought capable of overcoming its own self-centredness of belief, of admitting contrary beliefs and customs into the liberal stockade, of acknowledging the **principle** of **equality** in realms of life where human status and practices were so very different that the universalism of the principles of equality was sometimes very hard to apply (at other times, as when paying out wages to ethnic groups outside the usual membership, very easy).

Multiculturalism was the result, and it was teachers, as usual, who were commissioned by **society** to refine and transmit its lessons. They were helped in this by the literary theorists of so-called postmodernism who, tackling the new phenomenon of an English literature largely written by authors from all over the globe rather than the home country, came up with theories of 'difference' and how to accommodate it. They learned from anthropology the necessity to see others as those others saw themselves, how to represent strangeness in familiar ways, how to write not from within the membership of a 'knowable **community**' but in such a way as to honour and configure 'alterity' or 'otherness'.

In **education** this movement expressed itself in the decent policy of **inclusion**, although its policy practitioners became a bit evasive when faced by the fact and the **value** of membership of a living community, the definition of which is that other people be *ex*cluded from it. These problems had to be overridden. The old notion that immigrants in Britain could be assimilated like the masses who had arrived in the United States for the two previous centuries had perforce collapsed. Active integration of Asians, West Indians, Africans, East Europeans required political (and educational) **thinking**. The principles of liberalism which, with all their weaknesses, remain the bedrock of the British and American polities, adjusted themselves to 'pluralism', or the recognition and acceptance of social diversity.

multiculturalism

One key value in this process is tolerance, but the difficulty with this is that some counter-cultural activities, such as street drunkenness or blowing up commuter trains, *are* intolerable. Hence, multiculturalism has to parley with some kind of universal ethics and politics, and identify what social actions are impermissible because horrible. Liberalism dislikes this exercise. Nonetheless, in straining to perform it, it is proving the **truth** that **morality** has to change to meet historically unprecedented conditions. An ethics is now needed which matches the duties of a common citizen to the oddities of local **culture**. This will be, so to say, a politics of politeness, whereby difference is muted as a principle in exchanges with those who are very different.

This clears the important liberal test which insists on **individual freedoms** so long as the freedoms of others are not affronted. It does not do anything about the blank at the heart of liberalism and multiculturalism as to what constitutes good lives in their many diversities. Zygmunt Bauman dismisses multiculturalism, in a bitter joke, as a device on the part of the rich nations to get out of doing anything for the poor ones. What multiculturalism really implies is, he says, 'Sorry, we cannot bail you out from the mess you are in'.

FURTHER READING

Zygmunt Bauman (2001), *Community*. Cambridge: Polity Press.
John Griffin (1986), *Well-Being*. Oxford: Oxford University Press.
Amy Gutman (ed.) (1994), *Multiculturalism*. Princeton: Princeton University Press.
David Hargreaves (1990), *The Challenge for the Comprehensive School*, revised edition. London: Routledge and Kegan Paul.
Vijayendre Rao and Michael Walton (2004), *Culture and Public Action*. Stanford: Stanford University Press.

Needs

Needs are invoked with regard to children in what is often rather too ready, let alone too pious a manner. The important qualification is always to be able to tell the difference between needs and wants, and to confine the discussion of needs to certain basic requirements common to all human beings, including shelter, food, warmth, sex, loving-kindness and the sufficient company of others, safety, order. But as soon as such a list is nominated, there bursts out (and quite rightly) a clamour of dissent and elaboration: 'Oh, you can't miss out ...', and it is certainly the case that people come to regard as needful what started out, frequently, as a luxury. Most people would now think of telephones and television as domestic necessities, and it is true that in modern life, one could hardly know what is going on, and therefore function as a free citizen without these and other instruments. One might add that the same goes for an annual paid holiday; this now looks very like a basic need in the hardworking schedules of the industrial and service **society**, but such a thing was unthinkable to the workers of Victorian England and is meaningless to the starving millions of Africa.

To meet the fact of culturally various needs, the moral economist Amartya Sen has suggested that human needs be defined according to local circumstances; African, Chinese, Indian and European needs vary. The conditions necessary for free and adequate 'functionings', such that each person shall freely be able to exercise such fundamental capabilities as finding **work**, supporting a family, eating sufficiently, having access to the mobility necessary where each lives, making leisure and friends, enjoying **culture**, belong, Sen thinks, strictly to particular histories and geographies, and cannot be generalised. Any such list of 'capabilities' and 'functionings' should be drawn up by **development** agencies with an imaginative feel for what is best for people in the place in **question**.

Any such move would combine ethics with economics in a **theory** of human nature. The move is widely advocated by all the departments of the United Nations. But the academic debate on needs and **pedagogy** has largely been dominated by psychologists. Years ago C. I. Hull produced a theory of **behaviour** according to which a creature's body combined a series of 'drives' which the **individual** sought to keep in homeostatic (that is, self-correcting) balance according to **principles** learned for the purpose of drive-reduction.

This dismally reductive circularity proved quite inadequate to human motivation, and H. A. Murray invented a 20-part classification in which a sample of respondents to his Thematic Apperception Test wrote little tales about a group of pictures, from which Murray, in turn, derived his list of the motivations discernible in the narratives. These included such unexceptionable motives as aggression, deference, protectiveness, playfulness, and trying-to-understand, any one of which could have been mentioned in the most banal chat about why people do what they do.

Lastly, and influentially, A. H. Maslow produced, from his rather more exacting experiments with people, his 'hierarchy of needs'. This was a pyramid diagram rising from basic drives or physiological needs ('drive' and 'need' here being the same thing) such as hunger or sex, up the seven levels of the chain by way of 'love and belonging', 'needs for esteem', 'cognitive and aesthetic needs' (roughly the needs for **knowledge** and meaning), to 'self-actualisation' at the top. This latter included the 'realisation of one's full **potential**' (which can hardly count as a need and is, moreover, conceptually vacuous), and, in a forceful but also not very illuminating contribution to **teaching**, having 'peak **experiences**'.

Maslow's hierarchy is fine for animating discussion, but, in point of fact, human needs may declare themselves as motives in a quite different order from his, and some individuals seek out, say, **beauty** long before they look for safety. It may seem best, with Sen in mind, to match pupils' needs to the capabilities they can acquire and the functionings they must perform.

FURTHER READING

Len Doyal and Ian Gough (1991), *A Theory of Human Need.* Basingstoke: Palgrave.
Michael Ignatieff (1984), *The Needs of Strangers.* London: Chatto and Windus.
A. H. Maslow (1954), *Motivation and Personality.* New York: Harper and Row.
Amartya Sen (1999), *Development and Freedom.* Oxford: Oxford University Press.

key concepts in education

Norm

A norm (from which the adjective 'normal' is derived) is *either* the mean or average score in an aggregation of statistical results, *or* in sociological discussion it is a **principle** of social conduct, which may be moral, political or just customary. Driving on the left in Britain is a law; giving way to traffic from the right on a roundabout is a norm. Normality, of course, is the everyday but crucial measure of ordinary expectation, that which we take wholly for granted but the loss of which causes acute anxieties and, in the end, social breakdown.

Norms, as signifying customs and practice in everyday **behaviour,** are sometimes contrasted with **values** where the latter term identifies concentrations of meaning and significance, while norms are conventions regulating conduct but lacking moral or political force. What is normal is no more than habitual or, perhaps, a matter of politeness (although the etymological connection between politics and politeness is often overlooked). It is not clear, except to very rigid personalities, that what is normal must be complied with.

All the same, norms and normality are strong, implicit and necessary instruments of control. The Latin *norma* is indicative; it means a carpenter's square, for drawing and measuring. In statistics, by derivation, the 'normal curve' of the distribution of phenomena (people's height or weight or intelligence quotients) is a bedrock assumption upon which the **discipline** as a social science, indispensable to mass **society,** is founded. But the normal curve is a contingent discovery. It might not have been the case that human properties would fall into that pattern, and there is a natural tendency for social scientists, when they discover abnormal patterns of distribution, either to ditch them as inexplicable, or to force them into place on the normal curve.

In the human sciences, to refer to rules, actions or recommendations is generally to contrast them with statements of fact, so in such instances 'normative' has an evaluative weight. All modes of thought have their normative implications precisely because they select what is valid for a particular modality, and discard what is not. A valid inference is therefore something one *ought* to accept.

Among the numerous derivatives from norm, the word 'normalisation' refers simply to the restoration of routine and familiar provision after

sudden change, accident or violence. In an educational context, the use of 'norm' recurs in **assessment**, through norm-referencing.

FURTHER READING

D. S. Downie (1971), *Roles and Values.* London: Methuen.
Ian Hacking (1975), *The Emergence of Probability.* Cambridge: Cambridge University Press.
Ian Hacking (1977), *The Taming of Chance.* Cambridge: Cambridge University Press.
G. H. von Wright (1963), *Norm and Action.* London: Routledge and Kegan Paul.

Objective

'Objective' is used both as a noun and an adjective, unlike 'subjective' which is only used as an adjective (meaning personal to oneself). 'Objective' means external, for example, to describe a point of view that is verified by demonstrable facts, not just an opinion. As a noun, it means the object to be achieved, the end result of an action.

Few adjectives carry such a strong charge of self-approval. To be objective is, as far as personal matters go, to be detached, impartial (but judicious), dependably disengaged from the business in hand, and therefore able to appraise it properly. Objectivity, the noun, is counterposed to subjectivity, with the former indicating a truly scientific, thoroughly well-informed, but always distanced state of mind. Objectivity is the goal of science, whereas subjectivity refers to the warm, messy, sentimental but reassuringly human condition of the close-up, shortsighted and impulsive commitment in which we live day by day.

It may be suggested here that this opposition is a false one, and in educational matters should be discarded. Perfect objectivity of a moral, historical, or even scientific kind, presupposes a god's-eye view of life or, as Thomas Nagel calls it, 'the view from nowhere'. But all views are taken from somewhere. The philosopher Walter Heisenberg demonstrated, in his famous 'uncertainty **principle**', that even in scientific observations the results change with an alteration in the position of the observer. In some situations a subjective approach may be better prepared to comprehend human phenomena. Charles Taylor suggests that the best and fullest **understanding** of human predicaments is attained by enfolding them in a frame of feeling of the most morally sympathetic and loving-kindly sort, of which a particular interpreter is capable. This does not preclude natural feelings of, say, anger, when these are relevant.

It follows that the objectivity–subjectivity opposition might be muted in favour of the adjective 'intersubjective', as meaning the common world created by the collective efforts of the human mind. Any teacher might usefully notice the difference involved in thinking about things as '**subjects**' on one hand (that is, entities with purposeful attributes and meanings), and 'objects' on the other (that is, things to be observed with a degree of detachment and distance).

objective

145

For teachers, each lesson has to have a defined objective. To be clear about the desired 'end result' of a lesson sounds easy enough, but it is not quite that simple. The teacher might have the intention that all children in the class will have planned, or completed, a story by the end of the lesson. However, 'writing a story' is not the objective. It is the activity.

The following objective is taken from the Secondary National Strategy English strand 'Key Objectives Bank' for Year 8: 'Develop the use of commentary and description in narrative.' These elements will be explicitly taught, and pupils will then demonstrate that they have mastered these **skills** (or not) through writing a story. The objective refers to the skill to be learnt; the activity is how this skill is put to use. The end result may be writing a story. (Keep up at the back there!)

FURTHER READING

Thomas Nagel (1985), *The View from Nowhere*. Oxford: Oxford University Press.
Roger Poole (1972), *Towards Deep Subjectivity*. London: Allen Lane.
Charles Taylor (1985), 'Self-interpreting animals', in *Philosophical Papers*, vol.1. Cambridge: Cambridge University Press.

Pedagogy

The word 'pedagogue' comes from the Greek, meaning a trainer or teacher of boys. It is now an archaic word for 'teacher', and is sometimes used to suggest a rather pedantic teacher. However, 'pedagogy' is in current use, meaning the **knowledge** and **skill** that a person needs to develop in order to become a successful teacher. The National Strategies enlarge on this:

> Teaching is complex. Teachers and other practitioners draw on a range of working **theories** and their own **experiences** in arriving at their views on how children learn and how teaching can support this learning. There is an increasingly strong body of research evidence and practice that will help refine these views and inform pedagogical decisions. There are also many different definitions of pedagogy. The *National Strategies Documents* have developed the following working definition:
>
> *Pedagogy is the act of teaching, and the rationale that supports the actions that teachers take. It is what a teacher needs to know and the range of skills that a teacher needs to use in order to make effective teaching decisions.*

This definition is developed further into the 'four domains' of pedagogy, which are **subject** and **curriculum** knowledge; **teaching** repertoire of skills and **techniques**; teaching and **learning** models; and conditions for learning. This means that a teacher has to choose the best **method** to meet a particular learning **objective**, and also to tailor that to the needs of a specific group of pupils. There are numerous decisions that have to be made, based on knowledge of the curriculum, and previous **assessments** of the pupils. Different models will suit different situations. 'Conditions for learning' cover the atmosphere that the teacher creates in the classroom, through good relationships and stimulating materials. The aim, of course, is that pupils will 'enjoy' as well as 'achieve'.

FURTHER READING

Kathy Hall, Patricia Murphy and Janet Soler (eds) (2008), *Pedagogy and Practice: Transforming Identities*. London: Sage.
Jenny Leach and Bob Moon (2008), *The Power of Pedagogy*. London: Sage.
See 'supporting pedagogy' at: www.standards.dcsf.gov.uk

As noted in the entry on **individual,** 'person' is one of a set of terms for designating various versions of the social human being. Others include 'character' and 'self' as well as 'individual' in the most general categories, and a collection of other such individuations including 'genius', 'saint', 'lunatic', 'soul', 'ghost' and countless others, all of which are, so to speak, extra-social, that is they personalise human beings in ways which take no account of social roles or occupations such as parent, criminal, footballer or vicar.

Whereas a character has attributes and perhaps integrity, a 'person' signifies only another human being, although one with the **rights** and unignorable presence and actuality of all human beings, therefore never to be treated as disposable or as a mere thing or object. (Plenty of people would say that higher animals may be persons also.) Given this absoluteness, a person must be acknowledged as such, however awkward or unpleasant they seem: this is the keystone of liberalism, and must hold even when, as in the case of amnesiacs or sufferers from Alzheimer's syndrome, the brain no longer retains powers of recognition and association and, as people say, she 'is no longer the same person'.

To remain recognisably the same person, the philosopher Derek Parfit suggests that he or she must exhibit 'continuity and consistency' in personhood; that is personhood depends on a *connectedness* through time and across constituents (so I may have changed since I was 21 but I am still the 'same person'), and a sufficient consistency in characteristics (I am, perhaps, less cheerful or impulsive than I was, but these are changes wrought by my **experience** and leave me still with enough of the **qualities** I had in former times; or I can at least claim that my present qualities have grown consistent with my prior ones).

Out of these considerations comes the adjective 'personal' with its terrific and taken-for-granted forcefulness and bestowal of sanctimony. To describe one's reasons for doing or believing something as 'personal' is to warn people to keep their hands off; these are matters not for debate or dismissal. Given that the **idea** of a person has no particular content, only social reality and rights, the teacher is at pains to allow persons their own personality, but to show to the person which each student is, how to acquire and cultivate individuality; how to make of the fact of one's personhood a coherent character with a distinctive individuality (this is what it is to release and realise a student's **potential**).

In this process the individual person makes the discoveries as to **value**, possesses the experiences, feels the emotions and forms the beliefs, all of which are to be cherished as personal. But the most important lesson of the social, emotional and **spiritual curriculum** is to learn how to put the personal at a distance, and to understand oneself by way of an upright self-**knowledge** which honours but does not hide behind the value of the 'personal'.

FURTHER READING

J. S. Mill (1991 [1873]), *Autobiography*. Oxford: World's Classics.
Derek Parfit (1984), *Reasons and Persons*. Oxford: Oxford University Press.
Amélie Rorty (ed.) (1976), *Identities of Persons*. Santa Barbara: University of California Press.
Oliver Sacks (1998), *The Man who Mistook his Wife for a Hat*. New York: Touchstone.
Ian Suttie (1960), *The Origins of Love and Hate*. Harmondsworth: Penguin.
D. W. Winnicott (1965), *The Child, the Family and the Outside World*. Harmondsworth: Penguin.

person

Potential

To be 'potent' is to possess **power**; however, 'potential' refers to possible, rather than actual, power. It is something that is capable of emerging. This could be good or bad; a person might have the potential to be a criminal, or the potential to be a politician (or both).

In **school** terms, 'potential' usually refers to latent **ability**, which can be drawn out through good **teaching**, and by motivating the pupil so that he or she wants to do well. It is hard to develop a person's potential in every area. If someone practises constantly in order to become a tennis champion, he or she might be neglecting the potential to be a concert pianist.

The **inspection** schedule no longer refers to the potential of learners, although terms such as 'capabilities' or 'capacity' are used, which are equally hard to pin down; for example, it is not easy to predict 'learners' capacity for their future well-being' (using the evaluation schedule, September 2007, www. standards.dcsf.gov.uk/gender and achievement).

As 'potential' is something that is not yet realised, it is impossible to measure. Parents or teachers can only make guesses as to what a child might go on to achieve, if all circumstances, such as health, prove favourable. Potential can also be perceived to change, and it is affected by socio-economic status. For example, children who are assessed at similar levels in their early years are then at different stages by age seven – the middle-class children have pulled ahead.

FURTHER READING

Stephen J. Ball (2008), *The Education Debate*. Cambridge: Polity Press.
Office for Standards in Education: www.ofsted.gov.uk

Power

Nothing is more banal than to detect in the commonplace transactions of ordinary life the unacknowledged presence of, say, male power in the ritual humiliation of a wife, or status power when a university teacher puts down a student by sneering at her ignorance. Such incidents are real, repulsive and inevitable. But power in **society**, whether political or financial, whether carried off by the insolence of office or of inheritance, is also a social fact and the keystone of society. It confers **authority**; the state is the sole wielder of legitimate violence, and that violence – the police, the military, the prisons, the courts – is the ultimate expression of power, and the final sanction of the law.

So it is merely sentimental to point at power and make faces at it. The political theorist, Steven Lukes, acknowledges that power is intrinsically contested as a **concept**, that it is both factual and evaluative. He sorts between three dimensions of power. In the first dimension, power is exerted when the powerful compel the powerless to act in the sole **interest** of the former. In the second, more managerial dimension, power gets what it wants in more submerged ways, persuading and cajoling people who may not, it seems, know quite what they want in any case and are not being helped to find out. In the third, or 'radical' dimension, power is reciprocal and argumentative: human preferences may themselves be a product of a system which works against human needs and interests. The solution is critical and educative; it is to bring those wants and interests to articulation, such that people may decide for themselves what is best. This is the ideal politics and impossible of attainment. Nonetheless it is the classroom model of ideal **communication**, always there to appeal to, even if never fully realised.

Power is exerted structurally: by social **class**, by ethnic membership, by wealth, status and privilege. But it always admits of being brought to consciousness. It is held and exerted intentionally by men and women. Such exertion may be made symbolically (in customs, rituals, the public dramas of politics); may be made bureaucratically (the only possibilities are down on the form you fill in); may be made legalistically (in court you can't say or do anything outside the rules). In a **school**, power must reside with the staff. It is idiotic to pretend otherwise. But it is also the business

of the school, in the name, as before, of the great **value** of **freedom**, to teach the devices of power, its *negotiated* constitution, the unvarying lesson that only active self-government by citizens will hold off tyranny.

FURTHER READING

Hannah Arendt (1970), *On Violence*. London: Allen Lane.

Noel Entwhistle (1972), *A History of Progressive Education*. London: Routledge and Kegan Paul.

Clifford Geertz (1981), *Negara: The Theatre-State in 19th-Century Bali*. Princeton: Princeton University Press.

Steven Lukes (1974), *Power: A Radical View*. Basingstoke: Macmillan.

A. S. Neill (1995), *Summerhill School*. London: St Martin's Press.

Nicos Poulantzas (1973), *Political Power and Social Classes*. London: Verso.

Quentin Skinner (1981), *Machiavelli*. Oxford: Oxford University Press.

Principle

A set of principles may be counterposed to a **theory**. A 'principle' is in one meaning a guide or rule directing one's deliberations or actions. Thus, a person might say 'It is my principle always to back horses each way'. A principle may also be, however, something more like a foundation of one's personal integrity, as when someone says, 'It is a principle of mine always to treat my pupils as my equals'. Finally, a principle may constitute a guide to method, as in a celebrated book *The Principles of Literary Criticism* by I. A. Richards, which sets out what its author argues are the best rules for reading and judging poetry by close analysis of its constituent parts – rhyme, rhythm, **language**, form, tone. This is akin to **method** but more flexible.

In each of these meanings, a principle may be methodical, moral, empirical, political, scientific. It may recommend, methodically, 'always study paintings like this'; or, morally, 'always give away money you don't need'; or empirically, 'never depend on a hypothesis without 25 vindications'; or politically, 'no taxation without representation'; or scientifically, 'count, don't classify'. Scientific principles as found in nature, it should be added, are sometimes hard to tell apart from laws.

Principles, however, are not theories in that they do not yield explanations, although when propounded as **truths** ('nature abhors a vacuum' in science, 'you can't get an ought from an is' in ethics), one may go on to derive from the principle further truths. At the same time, certain principles, named by the philosopher Charles Peirce, 'regulative principles' may be no more than promissory notes; they direct us to what we hope to find is the case even though we may never do so. For example, some thinkers aspire to a theory of unified **knowledge** and conduct their work in the hope of finding or inventing it, but well aware that it may prove impossible. Some utopian planners have projected a **society** for the perfectibility of humankind, but know that it will prove very unlikely. These are regulative principles.

FURTHER READING

R. S. Downie (1971), *Roles and Values*. London: Methuen.
Clifford Geertz (1983), 'The way we think now', in *Local Knowledge*. New York: Basic Books.
Ernest Gellner (1964), *Thought and Change*. London: Weidenfeld and Nicolson.
I. A. Richards (1926), *The Principles of Literary Criticism*. London: Chatto and Windus.

principle

153

The original meaning of 'professional' was someone who had a religious calling, in order to profess one's faith. The word then took on a wider meaning, not just a **person** who joined a religious order, but one who had a particular trade or **vocation**. By the nineteenth century, the 'professions' had come to mean occupations generally carried out by the middle **class**. Today a professional is someone in a line of **work** that requires a specific qualification, such as a lawyer, doctor or teacher. There is also the distinction in sport between the professional, who plays a game in order to make a living, and the amateur, who does it for fun.

Recognition of the 'professions' was part of the coming-to-power of the British middle classes alongside the landed aristocracy in the nineteenth century. Merit, it was intended, would replace birth as the prime social qualification. Thus, the Civil Service was inaugurated with special **examinations** for admission; doctors were formalised as a distinct profession, also with systems of admission, examination, **career** hierarchy and supervisory hospitals; above all, the legal profession devised a new system, less fatally corrupt than its predecessor, with a **structure** of articled clerks, examinations of course, and, as with medicine, alignment with university departments.

By 1850, the institutionalisation of the professions was the mark of **progress** and confirmation of **power**. This being Britain, a hierarchy solidly entrenched itself, with lawyers and doctors at the top (the Civil Service in uneasy rivalry with them), and schoolteachers somewhere on the lower rungs of the ladder.

The word is used as an adjective as well as a noun. At its simplest, for example, 'professional footballer', it means getting paid – either earning vast amounts in the higher echelons, or not very much in the lower. In some contexts, and certainly in **schools**, it carries the meaning of reaching a certain standard of work, having the quality expected of a professional person. It also refers to **behaviour**; to be professional is to be discreet, and not to let one's personal **interests** interfere with the role. This is now widely used as a compliment (even if it sounds a bit boring) in many lines of work.

Teachers have 'professional **standards**' produced by the Training and Development Agency for Schools. The relevant document says that 'professional standards are statements of a teacher's professional attributes, professional **knowledge** and **understanding**, and professional **skills**'. A newly qualified teacher has to meet 33 identified standards, covering all aspects of the **work**. These statements are then used as a basis for 'performance **management**', and staff are entitled to 'professional **development**', which is training to enable them to improve – to meet, in time, the professional standards for 'excellent teacher' or 'advanced skills teacher'.

FURTHER READING

Mary Douglas (1988), *Can Institutions Think?* London: Routledge.
Michel Foucault (1974), *The Archaeology of Knowledge.* London: Tavistock.
Krishan Kumar (1988), *The Rise of Modern Society.* Oxford: Basil Blackwell.
Teacher Training Agency: www.tta.gov.uk

professional

'Progress' is another slippery term. Its basic meaning is to move forward, which implies improvement. However, taking this in its literal sense, one can walk forward into a bog, or over a cliff. To the Victorians, 'progress' meant that they were moving towards a more perfect world. Nowadays we are more sceptical, and we are aware that improvements can bring huge hazards as well as benefits.

Progress now takes its meaning from the advances of science and natural history which gradually led the people studying nature in the eighteenth century to realise that nature herself was on the move and not, as everyone had supposed, immutable. The scientist who finalised these discoveries and arranged them in his new theory of evolution was Charles Darwin, who published *Origin of the Species* in 1851. But for a long time, all the evidence had been pointing towards natural processes which developed in greater adaptation to the environment.

After Darwin's great classic came out, a movement began to apply his theories to history, and to discover in the progress of nations similar adaptation whereby 'the survival of the fittest' proved that those peoples with the greatest advances in wealth and weapons merited their superiority, and were entitled to make others their inferiors. 'Social Darwinism', as this repulsive doctrine came to be called, was disgraced by those totalitarian regimes in the twentieth century which sought to apply it, particularly Nazism and Stalinism.

Progress became an idea deeply entrenched in both political and domestic life. It is expressed in the common hope of all parents for the enlarged prosperity of their children, just as it is in every political party's manifesto. The idea of progress has, however, taken a battering in the twentieth century. As Thomas Hardy wrote in his Christmas verse for 1924:

'Peace on earth!' was said. We sing it,
And pay a million priests to bring it.
After two thousand years of mass
We've got as far as poison gas.

Since 1924, the advent of nuclear weapons, the invention of genocide, and the threat of natural retribution, in the form of flooding and fireballs from the sky, have diminished faith in progress, for all its universal appeal.

In school terms, 'progress' means pupils' progress, measured by National **Curriculum** levels. The expectation now is that pupils will move on two levels in each Key Stage, so should reach at least level 2 at the end of Key Stage 1, then level 4 at the end of Key Stage 2, and move on to level 6 at the end of Key Stage 3. This will not happen for every pupil. Progress is slower for lower attainers, while the higher attainers forge ahead. The gap becomes wider during their time in school.

For Ofsted, the definition of 'progress' is 'how well learners progress relative to their starting points and capabilities, on the basis of data and observed evidence, with any significant variations between groups of learners (for example, by ethnicity, **ability** or **gender**)'.

As an adjective in an educational context, 'progressive' generally refers to a type of schooling outside the state system, led by pioneers of progressive **values** such as Maria Montessori, Rudolf Steiner, and Bertrand and Dora Russell. They set themselves against the bad old days in which teachers were repressive and children repressed, and favoured such positive **qualities** as self-expression, **freedom**, creativity and **autonomy**. Their example did much to bring the lessons of progressivism to all schools and thereby add the glow of **vocation** to young teachers' **careers**.

FURTHER READING

Noel Entwistle (1972), *A History of Progressive Education*. London: Routledge and Kegan Paul.
Stephen Jay Gould (2007), *The Richness of Life*. New York: W. W. Norton.
Alan Milward (1984), *The Reconstruction of Western Europe*. London: Methuen.
Alan Moorehead (1969), *Darwin and the Beagle*. London: Hamish Hamilton.
Patrick Nuttgens (1989), *The Home Front*. London: BBC.
John Passmore (1970), *The Perfectibility of Man*. London: Duckworth.
Nicholas Timmins (2001), *The Five Giants: A Biography of the Welfare State*. London: HarperCollins.

progress

Like all interesting **concepts**, 'quality' has multiple and sometimes quite separate usages. One could start with its usage as referring simply to an attribute of a thing ('this rose has a lovely aroma') or a characteristic of a **person** ('she is a woman of great courage'). A quality or characteristic found in a person is also and generally thought of as a *possession* of that person, which is hardly how one would talk of the smell of a flower. Philosophers have made heavy weather of distinguishing between primary qualities, which are truly *in* an object, as hardness is in concrete or softness in a pile of cotton wool, and secondary qualities, which are the sensation or impressions – the **ideas** – we have of these primary qualities.

Such puzzles return us to the difficulties of ideas in philosophical idealism, and needn't detain us now. For the paramount contemporary meaning of quality is as an attribute with, implicitly, the adjectives 'high' or 'good' in front of it, as being those parts of life we most cherish and seek out. A young mother will speak of spending quality-time with her children, and mean by this that at such moments she and they will be able to share activity and give loving attention in a way the quality of which is higher and better because more complete and fulfilling, freer and more unrushed, than is normally possible in everyday routines.

This use of quality as in 'quality of life' extends widely, especially into social welfare, where careful evaluation and **judgement** is brought to bear on the quality-of-life of, say, the very elderly or the terminally ill. This gives rise in economics to important efforts to quantify quality-of-life without reducing what is measured to mere externals such as income per head or observable behaviours like physical health, hours in **school**, leisure time available to different social **classes**, amounts of consumer goods purchased. Quality of life economists, on the contrary, attempt to go deeper, and in the study of people's preferences (which is of its nature a study of 'ordinality' or the placing of preferences in an order, first, second, third …) try to determine how these preferences change with ease of fulfilment, how they match up to an **individual**'s sense of his or her personal freedom, to what extent preferences are shaped by common lifestyle, and what it is for a lifestyle to die out because people no longer want to live like that, or simply can't make a living on those terms.

Quality in this pervasive sense is everywhere, and has been much taken up in rather crude ways by educational managers. They have, on the whole, failed to learn from the quality of life welfare economists, and tend to think that quality in **education** is a matter of inspecting schools, lessons, **teaching** in terms of a few observables such as targets reached, class **discipline**, **'value added'**, teacher **competence**, student satisfaction (often calibrated from such crude indices as questionnaires with five point scales to be ticked), all added to a general impression taken in haste and paid for handsomely by the school concerned. A number of educational organisations have been created in Britain with deliberately corporate-sounding names, such as the Quality Assurance Authority, as part of a general tendency by all policy managers to apply the instruments and **ideology** of marketing and advertising to aspects of life where they don't belong.

No doubt all teachers and students want to be assured of high quality in what they do, but the **management** procedures of accountability or what is called 'transparency' are not the ways to attain it. Quality is, among much else, the product of a living **tradition**, of a deeply inculcated sense of **vocation**, of strong **principles** of **responsibility** learned by staff and students not under coercion but in **freedom** and relation to a vivid picture of the common good.

This is a counsel of perfection and yet it is widely upheld – upheld, say, by single teachers in remote village schools in Africa or Indonesia, and by the best of the profession at home in the hardest and roughest of British inner-city schools. Parents, pupils, teachers and inspectors all know the best when they see it. This is the meaning of quality.

FURTHER READING

Fred Inglis (ed.) (2004), *Education and the Good Society.* Basingstoke: Palgrave.
Martha Nussbaum and Amartya Sen (eds) (1993), *The Quality of Life.* Oxford: Oxford University Press.

quality

Putting questions and finding answers is the primary activity of the **mind**, and surely the defining relation of classrooms. But questioning is such a various activity for all human beings, that it is always worth recollecting D. H. Lawrence saying crossly to parents, 'When a child asks "why is the grass green?" it is really saying "is it really green or is it just fooling me?" and we prate on about chlorophyll and photosynthesis. Oh fools, fools!'

Not every question needs an answer; not every question deserves an answer. What the pupil learns under careful, restrained **teaching**, is to frame accurate questions when these are needed. Answers to questions can only be contradictory when they are answers to *exactly* the same question. If, to take an example from **art**, we stand in front of a picture and ask 'What does it mean?' the question is too vague to be answered. If we ask in the same vague way, 'Why does the painter make things look so weird? Why doesn't he paint things looking right?' again these are questions too loose to find an answer. Coming to **understanding**, and coming to a **judgement**, are like discovering the answer to exact questions. A statement or a proposition only makes sense as an answer to a question; **knowledge** is the result of inquiry. A logic in which answers are attended to and questions neglected is a false logic.

In order to understand any human action or a natural phenomenon, we put questions to it about the purpose and intention of the actor or about the nature and function of the phenomenon. Those questions must be detailed and particular. If one is trying to repair a washing machine which has broken down, one goes through the sequence of programme checking each unit. Checking each unit is therefore seeking to answer the question, 'Is this the part which has gone wrong?' If we find that it still works, we haven't failed to find the answer to the question 'Why won't the washing machine work?' we have succeeded in finding the answer to the question 'Is the water valve opening all right?'

Thus, agreement and contradiction, **truth** and falsehood belong to propositions intelligible strictly as answers to questions. On the whole, in conventional teaching, a proposition is taken to be a freestanding statement, with a **subject** and a predicate. However, by itself it makes no sense: behind it must stand the question to which it is the answer. Then knowledge accrues in a complex **structure** of such answers, and is to be comprehended by those using and **learning** it as answers to the right not the wrong questions, intelligent not silly ones. The recovery of such questions, whether in the human or the natural sciences is a historical matter, a matter of asking what questions the original scientists put in establishing the answers they came to.

As one would expect, experimental psychologists as well as paediatricians have paid a lot of **attention** to the way children respond to questions, as well as to what is going on when teachers put them. This latter point is of great moment: teachers need considerable self-awareness about the manner, frequency and type of their questioning. Pupils are very alive to variations in tone. They may well be distracted from a task by a new note in the teacher's voice, and be more concerned with what they believe the teacher is implying ('don't be so slow', 'can't you see what I mean?') than with the problem set.

By the same token, pupils may mean very different things by simple questions. They may be seeking more to please or to rattle the teacher than to find an answer. But broadly speaking, the teacher's prime purpose in the classroom is to teach, first, boldness and precision in the forming of questions, and second, a matching exactitude allied to comprehensiveness in the identification of answers. Cognitive growth, says Jerome Bruner, is a consequence of discovering questions which will, so to say, swing the pupil from an understood **concept** to a new and necessary one. The **quality** of the question asked will elicit the quality of the answer; it is only 'open' questions that will make the pupils think for themselves. However, questions with a fixed, definite answer have to be used sometimes, to check that some particular aspects of a subject have been learnt.

FURTHER READING

Basil Bernstein (1971), 'Language and social class,' in *Class, Codes and Control*, vol I. London: Routledge and Kegan Paul.

J. S. Bruner (1983), *Child's Talk: Learning to Use Language*. Oxford: Oxford University Press.

E. N. Goody (ed.) (1928), *Questions and Politeness*. Cambridge: Cambridge University Press.

D. H. Lawrence (1960 [1921]), *Fantasia on the Unconscious*. New York: Viking.

question

Responsibility is a **concept** and a **value** with multiple but intuitively well-understood meanings. Prime among these is probably its legal use, in which criminals or anybody else accused of committing a crime have to be shown to be responsible for the action in **question**, where responsibility takes in deliberate intention and purpose on the part of the miscreant, as well as moral capacity, **intelligence** and reason. It is a legitimate defence for a prisoner to plead 'diminished responsibility' due to loss of faculties or of wits; in everyday parlance, to hold **persons** responsible for something must mean that they knew what they were doing (or had failed to do) and were indeed capable of performing or not performing the action for which responsibility is attributed to them.

In legal and in moral history (and, because of both, in educational history as well) attributions of responsibility lead rapidly to decisions about punishment. The bitter arguments still being fought over the death penalty turn on questions of just or equivalent retribution ('an eye for an eye') for the commission of acts for which the accused was fully responsible. The big change in British values which comes through from the late nineteenth century teaches a radical softening of responsibility as the effects of such social conditions as acute poverty, parental or other brutality, ignorance and malevolence became better understood. As these causes were given greater weight, both moral and legal responsibility became attenuated and retribution was mitigated by the new technologies of rehabilitation and therapeutic treatment.

Legal argument is never far away from discussion about moral responsibility, as may be seen in the always fluid and uneasy roster of official school punishments and sanctions. The concept of responsibility is, more broadly, a keystone in our whole system of ethics, with the importance it assigns to **freedom**, **autonomy** and **rights** (the exercise and defence of rights assuming the practice of duties entailed by rights).

Thus, to be responsible for something is to have acted in full or sufficient **knowledge** of the meaning of the act, to have done so freely and in one's own name, and to be ready to answer for the likely consequences. In addition, as the lawyer Herbert Hart has pointed out, there are responsibilities enjoined by the social role a person occupies, a parent, say, or a teacher (whose role responsibilities are numerous and heavy). Nowadays, role responsibilities are tabulated by systems of **accountability**, according to which those who fail to discharge the duties assigned to them and fall short of the **targets** they were deputed to meet, are to be, in a hateful slogan, 'named and shamed', and subjected to the politics of blame given such self-righteous license by the national media.

It still seems better to stay with older versions of responsibility, whereby the public servants that teachers are, and like all grown-up **individuals**, understand the duties of their office, freely accept them and assume and acknowledge full responsibility not only for their not-yet-fully-responsible charges, but also for communicating the **idea** of full responsibility to those in front of them soon to be adult individuals and responsible citizens. There is a sombre little tale (an imaginary one) for illustrating a few of the difficulties in deciding upon moral responsibility. A young Englishman strays into a small South American town at a bad moment. Twenty Indian hostages are about to be shot as a reprisal of some kind. The executioner makes the Englishman an offer. If the Englishman will shoot one Indian dead, the other 19 will go free. If he refuses, they will all be shot. What should he do?

FURTHER READING

M. Foucault (1977), *Discipline and Punish*. Harmondsworth: Penguin.
H. L. A. Hart (1968), *Punishment and Responsibility*. Oxford: Oxford University Press.
F. Schoeman (ed.) (1987), *Responsibility, Character and the Emotions*. Cambridge: Cambridge University Press.

responsibility

163

It is sometimes said that the political arena has been swept bare of any agreed-upon **concepts** other than rights. The United Nations Charter of Universal Human Rights is nowadays taken as the measure of the just **society**, and **justice** has been situated as the paramount political **value** ever since Plato put it there 2,500 years ago. These rights derive strongly from the American Declaration of Independence in 1776 which 'held these **truths** to be self-evident' and assigned rights to 'life, liberty and the pursuit of happiness' to all men (if not women or slaves). Since then, the roster of rights has assumed a strong and secure form in all national constitutions and in the ordinary conversation of the **culture**.

Just how completely the **idea** of human rights may be grounded in necessity is much disputed. People are quick to claim a right to own an SUV or carry a gun, but it is obvious that there is nothing valid in such trivial claims. The legal philosopher Herbert Hart argued that the only natural right is the right to be free, but that should not be taken to mean a right to *act* freely in any way one chooses, only that one should be free, so to say, in one's being, that is, not arbitrarily locked up or compelled to think in alien ways or have life's necessities, like food or shelter, removed.

Probably it is as well to keep discussion of rights within a legal terminology. It is then the case that if one can prove a legal right, it follows that someone else has a legal duty to fulfil that right. If, say, I have a right to a job, someone else has a duty to provide me with one. In a **school**, the rules which establish **discipline** also confer rights: a pupil now has a right not to be struck by anyone, especially a teacher. More largely, the framework of legal rights is best justified morally; that is to say, rights ensure that a **person** has his or her best chance of well-being and free action when protected by a system of rights which so far as possible provide the best chance of attaining those goods. Naturally, for our rights to function properly, everybody must respect the rights of everybody else. For children, this is particularly crucial since children aren't usually large or important enough to stand up for their own rights, and the doctrine of children's rights, not very long-lived, is still fiercely contended, especially for babies (and, by extension, for animals).

This discussion of rights as legal entities omits two aspects of a many-sided topic. In the first, as argued by Simone Weil, one may object to the way rights have come to rule the political roost by spotting something selfish and curmudgeonly at their heart. Claiming one's rights is a nursery kind of reaction: 'That's my right', and Weil preferred, as a more absolute **principle**, that 'only good and not evil should be done to any human creature'.

The other objection to the rule of rights is that it obscures that different sense of the word which identifies right action: not 'What is my right?' but 'What is it right to do?' and it is noticeable that this latter sense of rightness of conduct is much observed by the first meaning. Right conduct is obviously the main principle of **morality** and follows from decisions about a person's duty or obligation as well as their preferences. **Questions** of rightness also arise in the definition of feelings ('What *should* I be feeling?') and desires ('What is it right to want?'), but largely the discussion of rightness pertains to everyday moral action and the rules and principles which direct them.

There are numerous moral schools, each with its own account of right action and how to decide what it is, summarised under morality. Here it will do to say in conclusion that most people nowadays feel the force of Kant's principle in choosing an action as right, that one is thereby justifying it as the right thing to do for *anyone* in that particular situation. This gives rise to the moral injunction that you should treat others as you would have them treat yourself.

FURTHER READING

Ronald Dworkin (1977), *Taking Rights Seriously*. Cambridge, MA: Cambridge University Press.
Alasdair MacIntyre (1967), *A Short History of Ethics*. London: Routledge.
W. D. Ross (2003 [1935]), *The Right and the Good*. Oxford: Oxford University Press.

right

Scholarship

The word has now a rather old-fashioned ring, at least in its general application. In its secondary (but widely used) sense, it denotes a special, usually monetary award to a student to cover the costs of courses at a **school** or university which would otherwise be difficult to afford. In its primary sense, however, scholarship refers both to a mode of employment and to a **vocation**.

As mode of employment, scholarship is the labour of all academic inquiry, exhilarating, patient, protracted, tedious. It is the application of the scholar to what used to be known as 'disinterested' study. But the word 'disinterested' is now, regrettably, shifting its meaning to something close to 'bored', where originally 'disinterested' meant, and needs still to mean, unself-referential, impartial, open-minded and non-partisan, weighing **judgements** without favour to a particular **interest**, seeking only truth, goodness and justice. Even though a **concept** may exist with no single word to enclose it, yet the dissolution of the word 'disinterested' into another meaning weakens this particular concept at the heart of scholarship.

For the mode of employment in scholarship is inseparable from its vocational hold. Being a scholar entails wanting to do the job. Meaning and practice are coterminous. The narrative signified by **career** is inherent to the scholar precisely because the scholar accrues **competence** only over time; his or her interests shape themselves gradually within the channels along which the **discipline** passes; only after time spent, both arduously and pleasurably, in making the necessary **progress** from A level and similar qualifications to undergraduate degree to Master's degree to doctorate, is the liberating secret of all **knowledge**, that it is diffuse, unbounded, *un*disciplined, thrilling, disclosed to the scholar. Only then, in the course of a career, does he or she discover the **freedoms** of inquiry, and yet must then, in the needful name of order and of the advances guaranteed only by specialisation and the division of labour, corral and mark out the new inquiry as a field, with a map of knowledge and its boundaries, landmarks, pathways and bearings.

Somewhere in his or her heart, the good teacher must feel the call of scholarship, its seriousness, its dedication, its comedy. Such a teacher must not forget how often the scholar is a ludicrous figure in literature, from Shakespeare's Holofernes to Ronnie Barker's mad scientist (although it is worth pointing out that few scientists, after lifetimes spent in libraries and laboratories, would actually call themselves scholars). Unworldliness is no use to schoolteachers, but if it is unworldly to prefer scholarship to money, teachers should do so. The pressure to magic knowledge into money is all around us, and scholars in schools have a duty to the future not merely to resist that pressure, but to transmute it into the common good.

FURTHER READING

Peter Abbs (2003), *Against the Flow: Education, the Arts and Postmodern Culture.* London: Routledge.

Pierre Bourdieu (1988), *Homo Academicus.* Cambridge: Polity Press.

G.H. Hardy (1942), *A Mathematician's Notebook.* Cambridge: Cambridge University Press.

George Steiner (2003), *Lessons of the Master.* Cambridge, MA: Harvard University Press.

scholarship

School

The word 'school' comes from the Latin *schola*, and a similar derivation has been adopted in nearly all European languages. The word means the actual building, but also refers to the institution as a whole – the building, the people inside it, and the whole organisation. This can be seen in sentences where the school seems to be a **thinking** being: 'the school is developing a policy' or 'the school encourages innovative **teaching**'. This type of construction, of course, conceals who is actually taking **responsibility** for these things. 'The school' may not be the perfectly homogenous entity that is implied.

As a verb, 'to school' means to train or **discipline**, for example in the schooling of horses.

Grammar schools set up in Elizabethan times were for the sons of the locals well enough off to pay the bill. The nobility employed tutors to educate their daughters as well as their sons. School was clearly not a pleasurable **experience** in Shakespeare's day, as he described:

> … the whining schoolboy, with his satchel
> And shining morning face, creeping like a snail
> Unwillingly to school. (*As You Like It*, Act 2, Scene 7)

Education provided by the state, as we have it today, developed slowly. In 1802, the Health and Morals of Apprentices Act required employers to educate apprentices in basic reading, writing and mathematics. It is interesting that the Act aimed to improve 'health and morals' as these are very much a focus for schools today, as shown by the current **inspection** framework.

Religious bodies started to provide elementary schools (basically primary schools) in the early nineteenth century. Provision was formalised in the Elementary Education Act (1870) and made compulsory in 1880, although fees were not abolished until 1891. Secondary education was still fee-charging. In 1902, the school leaving age was raised to 14. It was not until 1944 that the Education Act required all education **authorities** to provide primary, secondary and also further education. Systems are different in Scotland and Northern Ireland, but they had similar Education Acts at this time. By 1944, the school leaving age was 15, and then raised to 16 in 1972. Currently the proposal is to raise it to 18, although the time can probably be spent in **training**, not just in an educational establishment.

Schools now exist in all shapes and sizes, from the smallest rural primary school to the largest **comprehensive**, which can be well over 2000 pupils. 'Faith' schools exist alongside non-denominational schools. This is a legacy from the time when religious bodies were instrumental in setting up the first elementary schools. Schools can apply to be 'specialist' schools, for example, in technology, sport or performing **arts**. **Academies** now run alongside local authority schools. The different types of school are a key part of the government's wish to provide '**choice** and diversity' in education. However, there is not much choice for parents who live in a rural area with only one local school, nor for those who can't get their child into the school they want anyway.

As soon as schooling became compulsory, there were those who objected, saying it was an imposition, and a restriction on liberty. Schools where pupils had **freedom** in what they learnt, and how they learnt, were set up in opposition to state schools (for example, Summerhill), but of course these had to be fee-paying. Ivan Illich in *Deschooling Society* (1970) claimed that institutionalised schooling inhibited a person's will and independent thought.

Recently there has been a growth in 'home schooling'. Although education is compulsory until 16, it does not have to be carried out in a school. Parents can submit a plan to the education authority to educate their children at home. They have to follow an 'appropriate **curriculum**'. The definition of this will, of course, vary from family to family.

FURTHER READING

Pierre Bourdieu and J.-C. Passeron (1977), *Reproduction in Education, Society and Culture*. London: Sage.

Ivan Illich (1970), *Deschooling Society*. London: Sheen and Ward.

Michael Young (ed.) (1973), *Schooling and Society*. London: Routledge.

school

Skill

'Skill' has become another of undoubtedly key **concepts** used to cover so many different things that it is in danger of vacuity, that is, of having so many applications it means very little.

In itself, it indicates the accomplished application of a **technique**. A technique (from the Greek, *tekne*, which best translates as a craft) is a specialised, teachable **method** for the **achievement** of a specific purpose. It is subordinate to and an aspect of the deployment of a craft, which may be thought of as a coordinated battery of techniques. Thus, a skill is an accomplishment of a person directed to a purpose.

However, 'skills' have taken on a more recent range of meanings, according to which a skill is separated from **individual** human purposes. Along with 'technique', skill is applicable freed from personal intentions. In thus making 'skill' and 'technique' impersonally scientific, the coordinating framework of a craft is disintegrated, and skills are, so to say, demoralised. They are transcribed into the handbooks of technology.

According to this critique, each skill (that is, accomplishment or **competence**) is divorced from inner meaning; it is an outer attribute. This serves the **ideology** of what may be called 'technicism', which justifies a fundamental break between the knower and the known. This is a quite new anomaly.

The anomalousness is brought out by a well-known solecism: '**thinking** skills'. Imagine speaking the sentence, 'she thought skilfully'. This is nonsense. One may think, for example, quickly or pertinently, but these qualities of the thought are not the consequences of using a skill. A skill is instrumental, whereas thought (the **mind**) creates the instruments it needs to do its work. Logic is one such weapon. 'Thinking skill' is another gross progeny of technicism. It deflects **attention** from whether the thought is worthwhile or worthless, straight or crooked. It demotes **intelligence**.

'Thinking skill' excludes unenvisageable (but imaginable) ends. It therefore obliterates the imagination. Some people refer to **language** itself as a skill. To do so is to misunderstand everybody's natural capacity to speak completely new sentences. It is to become a parrot, copying other people's sounds. Language is an innate capacity, a human capability and the source of human **freedom**. It is a gift, like thought.

The two latter are inseparable, although not synonymous. Not to grasp these definitions is to make human creativity the creature of technicism.

Skill ought, therefore, to be reserved strictly for its limited designation: a particular accomplishment, achieved by **training** and facility, which is part of the armoury of a craft, itself always capable of transition to art or science. Thus, a tennis player, a nurse, a car mechanic, a financial adviser, a painter, a software engineer, a coal miner, a fashion designer, a parent, all possess (insofar as they are any good at the job) a range of skills, subsumed as the mystery of their craft. Their **knowledge** and their capacities are their own, put to the tasks of their employment. They are proud of their skills, which are irreplaceable. On a good day, they can turn skilfulness into **art**.

The best kinds of **education** effect this latter alchemy so that, from time to time, every student finds such fulfilment. When the drives of production go to **work**, however, they perpetually seek out new technology with which to supplant craft and art in labour. This struggle is found going on in the middle of the **concept** of a skill.

Schools now refer to 'key skills' and 'functional skills'. These are mere competencies, deemed to be the level required to cope successfully in a modern **society**. They cover **literacy**, numeracy and ICT. Children who entered secondary school in 2007 will, when they take GCSEs, be required to pass a 'functional skills' test in these three elements before they can be awarded a GCSE in the corresponding **subjects** (English, mathematics and ICT).

skill

An important consequence of the current of new **ideas** which swept Europe and North America towards the end of the eighteenth century and was known as the Enlightenment was a new awareness of the size and variety of the globe. This transpired in two ways: in the first, the new doctrines of **rights** and **equality** led thinkers to declare for the universal **principles** of human nature to be established in all societies; in the second, the voyages of exploration and imperialism, the new sciences of archaeology and anthropology, caused the recognition of the otherness and sheer difference of humankind.

As the nineteenth century advanced, it became obvious with the stupendous explosion of new technologies brought by the Industrial Revolution, in particular to Western Europe, that an unprecedented kind of society was in the making – a mass-producing, unstoppably manufacturing and multitudinous society moving in huge numbers from country to city life. Although there had been many theorists of the polity (or political society) before then, starting with Plato's *Republic* and reaching one of several pinnacles with Hobbes's *Leviathan* in 1651, another new science of society, eventually called sociology, was willed into being with which to explain the monstrous creature being born in London, Birmingham, Manchester, Leeds, Newcastle, Glasgow, Cardiff, Belfast (to go no further than the British Isles).

These sociologists and political theorists made a distinction between old, customary, traditional societies, still to be found in rural and peasant life in Europe until about 1950, and modern, industrial, more or less democratic societies, in which mass production, a high degree of specialisation in the divisions of labour and an amazing capacity to accumulate (but not distribute) wealth all flourished together.

The German sociologist, Ferdinand Tönnies, sorted between *Germeinschaft*, a society with strong **community** and ancestral feeling bound together by common implicit beliefs and shared modes of production, and *Gesselschaft*, a society of impersonal and contractual relations whose **principles** of solidarity were grounded on explicit rules, vast legal systems and bureaucratic **management**. Tönnies was followed by Emile Durkheim whose contrast between 'mechanistic' and 'organicist' societies was similar; mechanistic societies being held together by communal beliefs and mutual labour, and 'organicist' societies given order by their specialised divisions of labour, which divided people from the mutual practice and understanding of one another's **work**, but thereby bound them together in interdependence. Once upon a time, everyone did their own plumbing, carpenting, roofing, medical care and animal husbandry. Modern and differentiated societies have plumbers, electricians, doctors of a hundred specialisms, veterinarians for cows, sheep, poultry, llamas, kangaroos, kittens.

It was Karl Marx who, after the several European revolutions of 1848, saw that these divisions created separate social **classes** of very unequal wealth, and in a prediction which held many societies in thrall for a century and a half foretold world revolution and the eventual victory of the working class, or proletariat. As it turned out, he was mistaken and sociologists have had to study not revolution of a Marxist variety but nonetheless the transformation of the world by capitalist accumulation. This vast process has given birth to the many ingenious social, political and technological devices whereby the first societies to transform themselves into capitalist technologies in Europe and North America have battled, by way of innovation and suppression, to hold on to their position as the richest and most powerful nations.

It is the word 'nation' which provides one key to global competition. As societies came to consciousness of themselves as more or less a unity, they styled themselves *nations*, and as membership itself is compelled to do, pitted themselves against other nations. Held in precarious unity by their strong feeling for what has been called their imagined community, every geographic or linguistic or ethnic entity has sought for three centuries or so to achieve transfiguration from tribe, community, communion or people, to the status of a nation. In 1950 there were 50 members of the United Nations; by 1980, there were 158; there are now approaching 200.

At the same time, there are assorted moves towards transnational federations, the European Union being only the largest. Whatever counts as a society, the **concept** will continue to be expansive, porous, fissiparous, always in need of new theorisation if it is not to become vacuous.

society

FURTHER READING

Benedict Anderson (1983), *Imagined Communities*. London: Verso.
David Beetham (1985), *Max Weber and the Theory of Modern Politics*. Cambridge: Polity Press.
Marshall Berman (1982), *All That is Solid Melts into Air*. London: Verso.
Clifford Geertz (2000), 'The world in pieces', in *Available Light*. Princeton: Princeton University Press.
Anthony Giddens (1990), *The Consequences of Modernity*. Cambridge: Polity Press.

The National Curriculum enjoins that all pupils pursue their studies in such a way as to ensure their social, moral, cultural and *spiritual* development. As to what 'spiritual' either means or merely gestures towards, there is little common agreement beyond a general sense that it must be serious-minded, non-denominationally pious, giving rise to strong but not self-regarding emotion and quite often mixing mawkishness with doleful attempts to find a kind of universal theism hidden in various world religions and multicultural systems of belief.

There is nonetheless something humanly significant and decently reverent in the statutory insistence that spirituality be somehow taught and learned. Shakespeare makes Hamlet say to his friend,

> There are more things in heaven and earth, Horatio,
> Than are dreamt of in your philosophy (Act 1, Scene 5)

and the curricular effort towards spirituality is intended to enforce Hamlet's lesson.

The trouble is that, by and large, such efforts suppose strong feeling to be if not synonymous with spirituality, certainly inseparable from it, and further to connect spirituality with a more or less religious mysticism which (quite properly) has to show due respect for the varieties of religious **experience** without favouring any particular one. This is all the harder since Anglican Christianity, the official national religion, has become so little observed by most of the populace over the past 50 years, while other churches, especially of Islam, Jewry and more fundamental forms of Christianity, have become over the same period much more vehement in their allegiance.

In these confused and rather swirling circumstances, it is probably right that spirituality be expected to fare best in the context of religious art (as far as unself-referential emotions go), and in that of scientific discovery (as far as a cognitive vision of creation goes). This division of intellectual labour has the serious fault of confirming the view that the **arts** are all about feeling, and the sciences all about thinking, and such a division goes deep in our **culture**. The necessary correction to this is to take examples of the arts of a sufficient weightiness and grandeur (as matched to the age and **abilities** in the **class**): Mozart's or Beethoven's music, retellings of Homer or Ovid, the poetry of Wordsworth or T. S. Eliot, the paintings of Turner or Botticelli.

These are rather taxing and high-flying instances for most classrooms. But excellent art for **school** audiences is everywhere. The tricky part for the teacher is to try to show, on the one hand, that art is a serious route to the metaphysical thoughts which everybody has even if they don't know or fear the adjective, and that science, as the other key manifestation of human **understanding**, is only to be grasped by attentive movements of the **mind**, shaped by the right feelings of reverence, perseverance, fearlessness.

Cosmology, romantic poetry and painting, the study of pathology in illness or patterns of insect labour may all alike conduce to spirituality. If there is nowadays such a thing as a national religion, it is perhaps visible in the pensive pleasure brought to millions by trips to national parks, **beauty** spots and garden centres to pay informal homage to the beauty and plenty of nature herself. Given that nature is at last turning upon her mindless exploiters and threatening them with flood and fireballs, spirituality could well be taught as a redefinition of human attitudes towards a natural world and the universe beyond now inseparable from mind and culture.

The **inspection** framework requires a **judgement** to be made on pupils' spiritual development (lumped together with moral, social and cultural), but what inspectors are looking for in this area is very vague. Consequently, they latch eagerly onto lessons that encourage pupils to look beyond themselves – for example, through environmental issues – or to consider matters of life and death, as in a study of World War I poetry. Raising pupils' aspirations is sometimes seen as a spiritual matter: reaching for the stars. However, for many pupils, this translates into merely material goals.

The references below are not so much expositions of the **concept** as opportunities to find it in written practice.

spiritual

175

FURTHER READING

T. S. Eliot (2001 [1935–42]), *Four Quartets*. London: Faber.
Robert Goldwater and Mario Treves (1945), *Artists on Art*. New York: Pantheon.

Ted Hughes (1997), *Tales from Ovid*. London: Faber.

William James (1960 [1902]), *The Varieties of Religious Experience*. New York: Collier.

James Lovelock (1979), *Gaia: A New Look at Life on Earth*. Oxford: Oxford University Press.

Mary Midgley (2002), *Science and Poetry*. London: Routledge.

William Wordsworth (1850,1990), 'The Prelude', in *Collected Poems*. Harmondsworth: Penguin.

Standards

'Standard' first signified a fixed emblem, such as a flag. This was derived from the verb 'to stand'. The **concept** of a 'fixed point' can be seen in references such as this – 'the king's standard being the point of reunion of the army, and the centre from which commands are issued'. It thus became the fixed point to which comparisons could be made, so a **school** is said to have 'high standards' if results are above the national average, or 'low standards' if they are below.

Often, instead of being used in relation to a measurable point, the word 'standards' is bandied around to mean anything good, or whatever the writer happens to prefer, as in 'standards are falling' ('Crash! There goes another one!' as Ted Wragg used to say). 'Standards' are linked to the writer's own prejudices. Because the notion is then so vague, it is used to draw some astonishing conclusions:

> We've allowed so many standards to slip … Teachers weren't bothering to teach kids to spell and to punctuate properly … If you allow standards to slip to the stage where good English is no better than bad English, where people turn up filthy … at school … All those things tend to cause people to have no standards at all, and once you lose standards there's no imperative to stay out of crime. (Lord Norman Tebbit, Radio 4, November 1985)

Once you misuse your apostrophe, you are bound to end up in prison.

In current educational parlance, 'standards' are meant to refer to something precise, which is backed up by evidence. Usually the evidence is test or **examination** results, which are measurable and can be compared from one year to the next. Even when results improve, critics are not convinced that standards are rising, as they say the tests are getting easier. This is impossible to prove, because the style of tests and exams has changed enormously over the past 25 years. It is true that far more people get a C or above in GCSE English, for example, than used to do so, but critics do not accept that standards in English are higher (indeed, quite the contrary). However, they have to accept that standards are rising in information technology, as this did not even exist as a nationally examined subject 25 years ago.

In spite of its original meaning of 'fixed point', 'standards' is a slippery term, often depending more on opinion than anything. This is shown in a favourite phrase used by complainants and critics (usually of **comprehensive** schools): 'bog-standard'.

'Standard' is also used as an adjective, and in this use it tends to mean the norm, rather than a specifically high or low standard. For example, 'standard practice' refers to the most commonly followed procedure. 'Standard English' means the style of **language** that is most commonly used for **communication** across the country. Dialect speakers need to master standard English if they are to play a full part in the institutions of **society** as a whole.

FURTHER READING

www.standards.dcsf.gov.uk

key concepts in
education

Strategy

Like several other words currently used in **education** – for example, 'target' – 'strategy' has a military origin, meaning the movements and operations of a campaign. It also meant the plan for what was hoped to be a successful military action. In education generally, it carries the meaning of a long-term plan, the 'big picture', but the word is often used pretentiously. To be 'strategic' is a compliment used of someone who is, or is aspiring to be, a senior manager (he or she is obviously able to produce numerous action plans).

There are specific strategies, of which the most important is the National Strategy. This began in 1998 with the Primary Literacy Strategy, closely followed by the Primary Numeracy Strategy. These required staff to teach the '**literacy** hour' and 'numeracy hour' to a set pattern, and with particular approaches that were laid down. When it was discovered some of these didn't work too well, teachers were allowed to 'flex' the approaches. The Strategy was not statutory, but was policed quite firmly in its early days, especially in **schools** which had low **standards**.

Later, the separate literacy and numeracy strategies became the overall National Primary Strategy, and the various strands of the Key Stage 3 National Strategy became the Secondary National Strategy. This is meant to focus on Key Stage 4 as well as Key Stage 3. The main aim behind the strategies is to improve **teaching** and **learning**, and so raise standards. According to the Secondary National Strategy, a lesson should have a clear **objective**, a stimulating starter activity, explicit teaching of the **skills** required, an opportunity for pupils to use these skills in a practical context, and a 'plenary' – 'What we have learnt?' **Assessment** is another key element, and the National Strategy is producing various series of 'assessment focuses' which are criteria that teachers can use to mark work, and pupils can use to see how well they are doing.

'School improvement partners' are the latest idea to come from the National Strategy. Local **authorities** receive grants in order to deploy school improvement partners (SIPs) in primary and secondary schools. Each SIP has to be trained and assessed according to a national procedure. They are then required to spend five days a year working with a school (the five days include report-writing, as well as visiting the school). In this time, the school (in effect, the senior **management** team) has a 'single

strategy

conversation' with the SIP, rather than numerous conversations which would previously have been held with officers from the local **authority**.

FURTHER READING

David Middlewood and Jacky Lumby (eds) (1998) *Strategic Management in Schools and Colleges*. London: Sage.
www.standards.dcsf.gov.uk/primary strategy
www.standards.dcsf.gov.uk/secondary strategy

Streaming

Even in the old grammar **schools**, which were already selective, pupils were often put into 'streams'. These are teaching groups based on overall **ability**. Pupils quickly worked out whether they were in the 'top stream' or 'bottom stream'. It is a watery metaphor, and obviously the top stream was meant to flow more quickly.

The rationale behind streaming is that pupils will make better **progress** alongside pupils of similar ability, and planning a lesson will be more coherent, aiming it at a specific level. As with any system that categorises or labels people, there are problems. Some pupils don't fit neatly into a category – they might be good at one **subject**, but not at another. Making a decision on pupils at the borderlines is especially difficult.

A solution to these problems is a slightly different system called 'setting'. This recognises that a pupil might be adept at some **subjects** but not others, so he or she might be in a top set for English, and a lower set for maths. Some areas of the **curriculum**, such as personal, social and health education, might be taught in tutor groups, which are normally mixed ability. Setting is a fairer system than streaming, although it makes a timetable more complicated.

Comprehensive schools more often have setting than streaming, although some larger schools also have a system called 'banding'. This means a cohort of pupils is divided into an upper and a lower band before the setting takes place. This is virtually creating a grammar school and a secondary modern school within one institution, but not quite as divisive.

A recent review for the Scottish Council for Research in Education found some evidence in favour of setting young children for mathematics, but its overall conclusion was that 'there is no consistent and reliable evidence of positive effects of setting and streaming in any subjects, or for pupils of particular ability levels'.

Some comprehensive schools follow the logic of their organisation to its extreme and teach all subjects in mixed-ability groups. The rationale behind this is that higher ability pupils will spur the lower attainers along, and that no one will feel undervalued. It also means that teaching groups can be roughly the same size, without extra large top sets, and smaller 'sink groups' where all the badly-behaved children are put together.

Mixed-ability groups cause other problems, especially if the range is very wide, from the most academically able to pupils with **learning** difficulties. Teachers have to be seen to cater for everyone's needs, and to provide what is called 'differentiation' within the lesson plan. This can make planning a very complicated process. Classes in primary schools are usually mixed-ability, but are divided into smaller groups within the class. The teacher can end up giving five different sets of instructions for one lesson.

As well as catering for pupils with learning difficulties, there is concern about those who are 'gifted and talented'. (Gifted children are good at everything; talented children are talented in specific areas.) This group has to be 'challenged' or 'stretched'. However, it does not take the gifted very long to realise that if they finish their **work** too quickly, all they get is more work ('extension activities').

FURTHER READING

Brian Jackson and Denis Marsden (1962), *Education and the Working Class*. London: Routledge and Kegan Paul.

Brian Jackson (1975) *Streaming: an Education System in Minature*. London: Routledge and Kegan Paul.

Structure

Now one of the most respected words in the lexicon of the human sciences, 'structure' lends to its many theoretic uses something solid and well-made about its very sound. The **concept** originated in anatomy and was quickly borrowed by architects; in both cases, it refers ideally to the completeness of integration and the smoothness and dependability of articulation, in a body or a building. Physical anthropologists of the nineteenth century naturally borrowed it from anatomists, and it was obviously useful to the science of geology, which picked up speed after Darwin opened the way, and to the technology of heavy engineering.

It is hard to say whether the use of 'structure' to designate social organisation is a metaphor or not. There so clearly are empirical stratifications in **society** – of social **classes**, **genders**, generations and **identities** – the order and integrations of which are bolted together and braced one against the other not just 'like' but actually *as* structures; even if structures are implicit in custom and conduct, bodily demeanour and gesture. So, too, it is not merely metaphoric but actual to speak of the structure of a poem – a sonnet, say, with its 14 lines alternately rhyming within its three quatrains, all clinched by a final rhyming couplet. So, too, it is factually descriptive and not just metaphoric to detect the structure of a sonata, of a legislature, of the daily life of a rural village.

The general usefulness of the concept not being in doubt, therefore, it is worth remarking on the general weightiness of its presence in a discourse. To speak of structure is to speak responsibly, and yet one has said little more than that there is a discernible pattern in the matter on hand. The tricky part is then to draw the pattern: to fix the joints in one's plan of the structure, to determine what bears the load, to find its openings and closures, its spatial logic, its points of strain. The analysis of structure is then made to work for its living, and to move dynamically in social as well as physical **theory**.

As soon as it does, as is the way with social theory, it gathers ideological associations, and the doctrines of structural*ism* appear. Indeed, the first versions of structuralism appeared immediately after the confirmation of structure as characteristic of all nature whether in botany, geology, chemistry or physics.

structure

Freud and Marx, in their very different ways, believed they had discovered the deep structures of human nature, in psychology on the one hand, and economic history on the other. The psychoanalytic strata of id, ego and superego, the battle between the repressed neurosis and its 'sublimation' in civilised **behaviour** came together, Freud argued, in structures which determined all human conduct. So, too, Marx found in the creation of social classes after the invention of the capitalist systems of production and accumulation the essential structure of history as class struggle and its dialectical resolution in the dictatorship of the proletariat.

Both men, writing at the period of science's supreme self-confidence, saw structures as largely determinist, and humankind as impelled by them with only minimal control by human rationality and purposefulness. This inheritance was absorbed by later versions of structuralism, in particular in the **discipline** of linguistics, which at the hands of Fernand de Saussure, taught that **language** is a structure of signs and significations roughly corresponding to words and meanings, that these are held firmly in place by internal rules of application and figures of speech (especially metaphor and metonymy) which leave little room for any individuality of expression. In literary studies and even in ethics this contention gave rise to the concept of 'intertextuality', or the disappearance of text into context, summarised by the French cultural critic Roland Barthes in a famous essay called *The Death of the Author*.

No teacher can do without the abstract concept of structure (the structure of a lesson plan, of classroom organisation, of a whole school, of a society's inequality). Structuralism is important only insofar as he or she must come to some estimate of a person's **freedom** or destiny.

FURTHER READING

Anthony Giddens (1984), 'Structuration theory', in *The Constitution of Society*. Cambridge: Polity Press.

Talcott Parsons (1937), *The Structure of Social Action*. Glencoe, Illinois: Free Press.

John Sturrock (ed.) (1979), *Structuralism and Since*. Oxford: Oxford University Press.

A. R. Radcliffe-Brown (1952), *Structure and Function in Primitive Society*. London: Cohen and West.

Subject

The derivation of 'subject' is from Latin, *sub* – 'under', and *jacere* – to throw, so the original meaning of the word was a **person** under the dominion of a lord or monarch. It is still used in this way in the phrase 'subjects of the Queen'. It then took on the meaning of subject under consideration, so a topic or theme, and it is presumably in this sense that the word is used in the context of subject of a sentence. The word was used to mean the subject matter of an **art** or science from the sixteenth century onwards.

In **schools**, 'subjects' fill the slots on the timetable, the merry-go-round that pupils follow each day. Over the centuries, the subjects that are deemed important enough to teach have changed enormously, depending on what is seen as the point of **education** at the time; who is being taught and for what purpose.

In Shakespeare's day, the study of Latin lay at the heart of the **curriculum**. **Teaching** was based on the 'trivium' of grammar, logic, rhetoric, and the 'quadrivium' of arithmetic, geometry, music and astronomy. Constructing arguments (in Latin) was an important part of the pupils' practice of rhetoric. They were expected to imitate different writers. The contrasting styles of the funeral orations of Brutus and Mark Antony in *Julius Caesar* show the rhetorical **skills** that Shakespeare would have learnt at **school**. Perhaps the nearest equivalent nowadays is the focus on 'writing to persuade, argue, advise' in the English curriculum.

Gradually, subjects began to exhibit common characteristics: a particular method of inquiry, a tradition of ordering **principles**, a distinctive idiom or typical way of talking, an identifiable subject matter, an accepted list of classic texts and scholarly ancestors. Once a subject has won these things for itself, it also acquires university and school departments, special shelves in the library, degree courses and GCSE or A level labels. It also provides its students with intellectual **identity**; they develop subject-loyalty. They patrol the boundaries of the subject, chasing out trespassers ('He can't do that; he's not really a physicist').

There are great strengths in such loyalties, but they may imprison **minds** as well. For a time in the 1970s, there was a marked loosening of these boundaries in both schools and universities; 'studies' replaced '**disciplines**'. This caused loss of identity, leakage across the boundaries and

subject

185

uncertainty of method. The difficult (but exhilarating) task is to have things both ways: to be sure of your **tradition** and its **method** and **principles**, and to carry them openly into the many unmarked fields of thought and inquiry, as yet unexplored.

The struggle over the forms of knowledge is endless, and the National Curriculum is one of its battlegrounds. The National Curriculum has to be followed by pupils up to the end of Key Stage 3, consisting of 16 subjects. Many of them are the same as those taught at the beginning of the twentieth century, although 'drawing' has become art and design, 'singing' is now music, 'scripture' is religious education, and woodwork (for boys) and cookery (for girls) have become design and technology, with its numerous components. Some new subjects have been introduced, such as information and **communication** technology (ICT), **careers** education, **work**-related learning, **citizenship** and personal, social and health education. These last two are key elements in the government's desire that schools should turn out upright citizens who play a full part in a democratic **society**, and do not become pregnant too soon, or obese.

There are other subjects which are not part of the National Curriculum but which may be studied in school, for example, drama and media studies, both spawned by English.

At Key Stage 4, new 'vocational subjects' are offered at GCSE, such as business, engineering, health and social care, leisure and tourism. These are geared to the world of **work** and include visits or placements in industry or business, to gain some practical **experience** of the skills used. Students can **progress** from these to vocational A levels or modern apprenticeships. Vocational qualifications are meant to have equal status with academic subjects, although there is suspicion in some quarters that, after the age of 14, a different curriculum is developing for the worker bees from the one for traditional academic students.

FURTHER READING

Bernard Sharratt (1982), *Reading Relations: The Structures of Literary Production.* Brighton: Harvester Press.

Geoff Whitty and Michael Young (1978), *Explanations in the Politics of School Knowledge.* Peterborough: Nafferton Press.

Sustainability

The verb 'to sustain' came into English from the French *soutenir* (in Italian, the verb is *sostenere*). It means to keep a **person** or a **community** from failing; or to cause something to continue at its existing level or standard. The word has been used in this way since the thirteenth century.

In **schools**, good results have to be sustained (and, if possible, improved). Staffing levels have to be sustained, depending on the budget. Sustainability, in these contexts, relies on the school's capacity to keep going at the same level. If a specific **training** initiative is in place leading to a new **strategy**, the school has to be sure there are enough trained staff to take this forward – to ensure its sustainability.

However, 'sustainability' now has a meaning in relation to the wider environment, indeed to the planet itself. How sustainable is our way of life? Pupils will have to consider this in **citizenship**, and they will meet the **concept** in science. The most ecologically responsible schools put it into practice – for instance, by providing renewable energy for the school through their own wind turbine, or by solar panels.

FURTHER READING

George Monbiot (2007), *Heat: How We Can Stop the Planet Burning*. London: Penguin.
Eco-Schools: ecoschools.org.uk
Generation Green: generationgreen.co.uk
ncsl.org.uk/sustainableschools
Sustainable Development Commission sd-commission.org.uk
Sustainable Schools National Framework:teachernet.gov.uk/sustainableschools/framework

Targets

'Target' has military connotations, and is one of the terms adopted by the world of **education** that has a combative sound – for example, 'drive up **standards**'. Targets have to be 'challenging'. They are set at different levels – whole **school**, **individual** teacher (for his or her classes), and individual pupil level.

Target-setting has become a central practice for the measurement of success in large corporations since the 1970s. Departments were set sales and productivity targets according to certain **theories** of **management**, and rewarded accordingly if they reached them.

This procedure was then imported into public services, including both the NHS and schools, during the 1980s. At the same time, schools were assigned individual budgets and separated from local **authority** funding. The controlling **idea** was that schools should compare themselves with one another like business enterprises, that their performance in meeting targets should be published in league tables, and that these results should be the criteria of success. The result was that schools endeavoured only to meet targets, and therefore neglected broader matters of education. This, as noted elsewhere, is a danger intrinsic to systems that subordinate trust to **accountability**.

Departments for children's services have targets in numerous areas, such as **examination** results (which should be set high) and teenage pregnancies (which should be low). The government sets itself targets for national outcomes. School targets are set using data on pupils' prior attainment. However, targets should not be confused with predictions. For example, a pupil who attained level 5 in English tests at the end of Key Stage 3 might be predicted grade C in GCSE English, but his or her target would be a B grade. A prediction is what pupils are expected to achieve if they continue on an even trajectory; a target in what they will achieve on a good day, with a following wind and plenty of 'booster classes'.

The current system of target-setting is similar to the nineteenth-century government policy of 'payment by results', where narrow and rigid testing for each pupil was applied by inspectors.

FURTHER READING

www.standars.dcsf.gov.uk/target setting

Teaching

The verb 'to teach', and its irregular past participle 'taught', go back to Old English, with the meaning to show, to instruct, to impart **knowledge**. This implies another **person**, or other people, who are being instructed. Teaching cannot be carried out without learners – whereas **learning** can be carried out without teachers.

Teachers do not have to be paid **professionals**. Babies and young children are taught by their parents to talk, and to take part in numerous activities. Children are taught all kinds of things (desirable and otherwise) by other children. Ever since Plato, there has been an argument as to whether **society** should pay a special class of professionals to teach, train and socialise its children. Plato certainly believed there should be such an officer, and he is generally counterposed to the eighteenth-century revolutionary, Jean-Jacques Rousseau, who was the first to believe that education should be a process of natural absorption and should follow the rhythms of a child's **interest** in the world.

In **schools** today, teachers are urged to use a variety of 'teaching styles'. This is to ensure that pupils are kept interested and busy. Styles include different **techniques** for discussion, asking **questions**, group work, drama and role play, and, nowadays, different approaches using the interactive whiteboard. The craft of teaching, usually in this case by professionals, is also referred to as **pedagogy**. Teachers are trained in **skills** and techniques, but the way they deploy these can make teaching an **art** (as described in the introduction to this book).

The meaning logically intrinsic to the concept entails that for anyone to be said to be teaching, it must follow that someone else is learning. Moreover, as is said in the introduction, while teaching certainly has its special collocations of techniques, it is, at its most resourceful, an art, which is to say the expression of creative power and its **communication** to other people. Naturally, practice only rises to the level of art on occasions, and teaching may often be routine, drilled, repetitive, and is invariably tiring. But it is an intrinsic and life-giving human activity, and to be honoured accordingly.

FURTHER READING

Maurice Galton and John MacBeath (2008), *Teachers Under Pressure*. London: Sage.
Gilbert Highet (1962), *The Art of Teaching*. Oxford: Bodley Head.

Tekiné is Greek for the application of a particular **skill** in the practising of a craft. In the practice of a craft, the craftsman is directing applicable skills towards a specific end already known and envisaged. In the making of a **work** of **art**, on the other hand, the artist will only know what he or she has made when it is (near enough) finished. It will be more like a discovery than a completion. The philosopher R. G. Collingwood wrote that 'True expression is an activity for which there can be no technique', the point of a technique being that it enables someone precisely to repeat what has been done before.

This is obviously important. There are set techniques for handling a computer, for instance. The novice needs to learn them if he or she is not to make wasteful errors by trying to start again from scratch ('reinventing the wheel', in the cliché). Everyone must learn the techniques which build on the **learning** and the inventions achieved by previous generations. That is one main function of **schools**.

The trouble is that science and its servant, technology, has for at least three centuries been so successful in inventing new instruments with which to simplify techniques (in manufacture, in reproduction, in **communications** media, in all social organisation), that it has come to be supposed that there are techniques for *everything*, that all human activity may be shaped and smoothed by new technologies, and thereby made foolproof.

What is proof against fools, however, is also unamenable to novelty or to new purposes. A technique resists **individual** application. This is apparent in the steady reduction of the artistry in the art of **teaching**. New techniques are not only commended but legislated which systematically reduces the importance of living **persons**, with all their oddity and originality, doing their teaching on behalf of the 'unenvisageable end' which is an educated **person**. This is the error which makes talk about 'fulfilling **potential**' so fatuous.

Critics of the unstoppable advance of purely instrumental **thinking-and-doing** (which is another way of saying 'technical **education**') have named such an **ideology** 'technicism'. For all the indispensable advances and creations of new technology, it remains in some large part a menace to human creativity and resourcefulness, leading people to believe that there are techniques for resolving all personal difficulties, whether sexual, moral, political or physical.

'Technicism' is the victory of means-end thinking. It makes impossible that vital movement of thought which is only completed when one says to oneself, after many false starts and detours, 'Yes, that's it. *That's what I was after'*.

No one can ignore the technical advances of a civilisation – to try to do so would be madness – but equally no one should suppose that there is a technique for solving all puzzles. This is the fatal error of instrumentality as a frame of **mind**.

What true art and good science have in common is the determination to make discovery precise, to create exactitude. Techniques on the way to achieving those goals do not define that end, but only lend useful aid in approaching it. Keeping techniques in their proper place is of a piece with knowing a skill for what it is. Techniques and skills are merely the tools of the **mind** and it is the mind and character of the person, the **imagination**, cognition, reason, using them which count.

FURTHER READING

Theodor Adorno and Max Horkheimer (1979), *The Dialectic of the Enlightenment*. London: Verso.

Hannah Arendt (1958), *The Human Condition: A Study of the Dilemmas Facing Modern Man*. Chicago: University of Chicago Press.

John Passmore (1970), *The Perfectibility of Man*. London: Duckworth.

technique

At its most straightforward, a theory is an explanation proposed of a particular problem, and the test of it is whether the explanation holds up. A theoretic explanation of a social action is therefore, in common parlance or in academic history, a story about what is going on which seems to fit the facts and provide for our understanding of the events in **question**.

In the thirteenth century, an English Franciscan monk called William of Ockham enunciated his so-called '**principle** of parsimony' (or 'Ockham's razor') according to which any explanation should ruthlessly cut away any superfluous detail and confine itself to the simplest and most reductive terms possible. This recommendation will hold good for all forms of explanation, whether in the human or natural sciences. Ockham's first precept translates from the Latin roughly like this: 'entities [in explanations] should not be multiplied any further than strictly necessary'. You have only to listen to the crazy over-invention of motives and intentions attributed to other people in customary gossip to feel the force of Ockham's rule.

A useful theory is, therefore, the thriftiest form of explanation, yielding **understanding** and, in natural science, predictive power. In scientific **method** a theory is constructed on the basis of a hypothesis which is then tested and retested either until falsified or until it is reckoned strong enough to grant 'permission to proceed'. The hypotheses thus experimentally tested then yield axioms from which are deduced the natural laws governing the phenomena. Naturally, the best theories are those which bind together the results of the largest number of tested hypotheses.

Tough-minded theories of science look for explanatory and predictive models which issue in 'grand theory', but more recently, in the face of more and more complex and contradictory data, especially in biogenetics, scientists have softened the demands made of hypothetico-deductive method, and settled instead for the more informal application of theory to more limited areas of empirical inquiry.

This leaves them on the wrong side of the line between description and explanation which is supposed to mark the distinction between the natural sciences and their system of predictive laws, and the human sciences, which have to settle for reasons not causes, interpretation (soft) not explanation (hard). There seems, therefore, to be something of a convergence between the two kinds of theory. However this may be, historical or sociological theory must certainly remain satisfied with interpretation (hermeneutics, as Aristotle called it), or what Clifford Geertz calls 'thick description'. This is hermeneutic method, which is to study as clearly *and* as imaginatively as possible the public conduct of human beings in action, and to identify as best the interpreter can the reasons, motives and intentions of those people, found in what they wrote, thought and did, thereby to map 'the constellations of **ideas**' enshrined in their history.

'Thick description' thereby yields a theoretic interpretation peculiar to the action in question. There are no general laws of human nature.

FURTHER READING

E. H. Carr (1965), *What is History?* Harmondsworth: Penguin.
Clifford Geertz (1975), *The Interpretation of Cultures*. New York: Basic Books.
Karl Popper (1967), *The Logic of Scientific Inquiry*. London: Routledge and Kegan Paul.

theory

This is another of those commonplace words which are as crucial to **education** as to life, but which are so various and so elusive it is hard to be sure what they mean. To begin with, one can say that thought and thinking cover everything which happens in the **mind**: reasoning, feeling, dreaming, analysing, meditating, doubting, cogitating … the list goes on for ever. Yet it can make perfectly good sense for someone to say to us, 'When I did that, I wasn't really thinking'.

So 'really thinking' perhaps indicates a more conscious and applied activity of the mind than images and impressions just drifting through one's head. Thought of this kind has a **subject**, or perhaps preferably, it has an object. Now at once we have a complicated puzzle for thinking to sort out: what is the relation between subject and object? In grammar, the answer is easy. Every whole sentence has a subject, as in 'John is running', where John is the subject, which is to say the active noun in the sentence. Every sentence with a finite verb in it has an object, as in 'John is buying his tea', where 'his tea' is object to John the subject. (Things get more complicated when the verb in question is 'to be', which is not finite, but that need not delay us here.)

In grammatical analysis, subject and object are distinct. In thinking, they are not. The philosopher Kant made a distinction between objects (or things) as perceived and objects (or things) *in-themselves*. The first is a phenomenon (that is, we know it through our senses); the second, which we can never know, is the thing as it is. His rival, Hegel, took this argument much further, contending, first, the **identity** of consciousness with its object, and second, the identity of consciousness with one's developing **knowledge** of one's self. This process Hegel further embedded in the collective coming-to-consciousness and therefore coming to self-knowledge of the human mind in general. **Progress** for him was the realisation of the human mind as itself and as rational.

The honest teacher at this point might well say in bewilderment, 'But what has all this stuff to do with thinking and therefore with education?' The answer is that, abstruse as these arguments seem to be in a brief summary like this one, Kant and Hegel were part of 2500 years of trying to determine what thinking is and how to do it. Plato was pretty well first into this field, and his answer to the subject–object distinction was his metaphor of The Forms, whereby all our perceptions (or 'apprehensions') are no more than the shadowy outlines of a system of ideal forms which human life is too transitory ever to behold in their immortal perfection.

The way to hold in balance the many theories with which thinkers have tried to stabilise the subject–object distinction at the heart of thinking is to grasp them historically. Different epochs conceptualise the question differently. Our own epoch, dominated by science, tries to objectify absolutely. It can't be done.

Not that the subject–object relation is the last word on thinking. It is most natural to think about thinking in terms of **language** and speech. For ordinary introspection shows us that thought may precede speech, that the body itself is thinking (the gut blushes and goes pale like the face, skin surfaces contract and quiver when one is frightened, blood pressure shoots up in rage). Even when the effort to think is strictly mental (if that is ever the case), we all know what it is to put into words the thought we have, and then to be quite sure that these words do *not* say exactly what we mean. 'No, no,' we say, 'that's not it,' and then we try to rephrase our thought so that we have it clear in language.

When it *is* clear, we know it for sure. The word 'clear' is just what we mean, as when we come into a sunlit clearing out of the darkness and density of a wood (the image belongs to the German philosopher, Heidegger). The readiest examples of this process which we have to hand are the manuscripts of poets as they wrestle with the words, cross them out and substitute others, until they know what they mean by having written it down. They are not merely embellishing the original thought with decorations; they are *discovering* what they think. Genius, it has been said, is the capacity to handle and transform the wordless states of feeling and apprehension into novel images or metaphors for understanding the world, *before* the deadening weight of cliché has a chance to nullify them.

This is thinking before the rules exert their **power**, and it would be grotesque to belittle, say, the essential rules of logic or the **principles** of induction. They are the grounds of rationality and only a lunatic ignores them. But it was Shakespeare who wrote:

> The lunatic, the lover and the poet
> Are of imagination all compact … (*A Midsummer Night's Dream*, Act 5, Scene 1)

thinking

and any discussion of what it is to think at all, especially with regard to children, should treat lunacy with due respect.

FURTHER READING

Simon Blackburn (1999), *Think*. Oxford: Oxford University Press.
D. W. Harding (1970), *Experience into Words*. London: Chatto and Windus.
Thomas Nagel (1997), *The Last Word*. Oxford: Oxford University Press.
W. V. O. Quine (1960), *Word and Object*. Cambridge, MA: Harvard University Press.
Gilbert Ryle (1979), *On Thinking*. Oxford: Oxford University Press.

Tradition

In everyday conversation, a tradition means hardly more than a local custom or a little ritual which is consistently re-enacted by a particular group, and serves as a nexus or collecting-point of cherished memories, whether of people or places, special dates or well-loved practices.

Such a meaning is strong and sufficiently close to the origins of the word in the Latin verb whose past participle translates as 'what is handed on'. This sense of tradition is, however, rather an inert one. Tradition becomes something from the past which is endlessly repeated but which does not discharge any of its energy into the present. By this token, to be a traditionalist (which everybody wants to be in some part of themselves) is simply to call up the past and replay it. It is sometimes alleged that this is what a political conservative is, and indeed the British Conservative Party used once to make great play with its ownership of, and reverence for, tradition.

Tradition is, however, a larger human necessity than the property of a single political party, although all such parties have and conserve their traditions. It is a banal enough observation that without 'the thread of life' to lead us from past into future **experience** we would be out of our **minds**, and since every institution is the product of human beings' collective thought, the same is true of the ordering of **society** in all its traditional aspects.

This latter argument is obvious when we consider **schools** themselves. A school has its own 'thread of life' which it symbolises in its traditions. Speech days, honours' boards, badges of office, school prizes, sports colours, old pupils' associations, school assemblies, were once the signs of cultural continuity and generational membership for local schools. But tradition as endorsed by such emblems and customs has over the past three or four decades become looser and less visible, and schools now root their continuity in the more informal practices of school festivals, theatrical performances and concerts, sports days and the like. This makes for a weaker school **identity** and a corresponding thinness of tradition, itself a consequence of the radical individualisation of common social experience. It is compounded by the much greater mobility of school staff, such that there are many fewer long-serving members of staff and, therefore, much shorter institutional memories. For the good headteacher and his or her school the making of tradition is crucial and very difficult.

There is also a stronger and more pervasive account of tradition as essential to holding a social order in place, and that is a tradition conceived as a commonly understood form of practical rationality. In this meaning, tradition is embodied in the best practice of a way of doing something. Thus, a gymnast or a pianist or a mathematician, practising those arts and crafts in a school, learns to distinguish between what is good for each of them in their present circumstances, and what is good unqualifiedly. They were apprenticed to a practice, and acquire the habits of **judgement** and action which **discipline** and redirect their unformed application and desires until, in the practices of gymnastics, piano-playing or maths, they are moved only by those reasons for action which transpire as being good at the **subject**.

These are each a form of practical reasonableness, and to be reasonable in one's practice is not only to become a practical member of a tradition, it is also to uphold and perpetuate a social **structure**, in our examples the social structure of **education**. Insofar as that structure is built out of a medley of intersecting 'practical rationalities' it will also integrate a shared picture of a form of life which is the best common life imaginable to the school at a given moment.

FURTHER READING

T. S. Eliot (1920), 'Tradition and the individual talent', *The Sacred Wood*. London: Methuen.

Basil Bernstein (1975), 'Ritual in education', in *Class, Codes, Control*, vol 3. London: Routledge and Kegan Paul.

Alasdair MacIntyre (1998), 'Practical rationalities as social structures', in Kelvin Knight (ed.), *The MacIntyre Reader*. Cambridge: Polity Press.

Richard Wollheim (1984), *The Thread of Life*. Cambridge: Cambridge University Press.

Training

As with **teaching**, training involves passing on **skills**, from someone who has already acquired them to someone who hasn't as yet. Training animals is different, as the trainer may not possess the skills himself (or may not want to balance a ball on his nose, nor jump through hoops), but he has the blueprint of the skills he wants the animal to learn. 'Training' can imply drilling and repetitive activities, as in training for fitness.

Professional training is to equip the trainee with the skills necessary for a particular profession. Initial teacher training (ITT) may sometimes seem to the trainee to involve drilling and repetition, and perhaps also jumping through hoops. In the past, teaching was seen as an intuitive activity; good teachers were born, not made. Now the view is that the skills can be learnt, especially if trainee teachers follow set structures for lesson planning and **assessment**.

Teachers are entitled to training throughout their **career**, so that they can continue to improve. The argument is that however good you are as a teacher, you can always be better.

In the past, training invariably meant 'going on a course'. Some of these were useful, some not so much. The preference now is to tailor the training to the **individual**, and to the **school**. This can mean buying in consultants who will offer exactly what is wanted, or else using expertise already within the school. Currently, a popular approach is 'coaching', where teachers within a school are paired together. The coaching may focus on one specific aspect of **pedagogy**, and the teachers may not necessarily be in the same department or primary year group. The process is non-judgemental and can involve questioning, observing, giving feedback, and modelling. A variation of one-to-one coaching is peer coaching in which a small group is given time in school to observe each other teaching, and discuss the **experience** together. This kind of training encourages openness and honesty.

FURTHER READING

Sara Bubb and Peter Earley (2007), *Leading and Managing Continuing Professional Development*. London: Sage.

The pursuit of truth is named as fundamental to any account of **knowledge**, and is, therefore, intrinsic to all systems of **education**, let alone systems of religious or ethical belief. Yet 'truth' is a word likely to cause embarrassment among many people, perhaps especially teachers, if it is invoked as the (or a) point of some part of the **curriculum**.

Unease of this kind is not without its justification, since nothing is more fruitless in intellectual discussion than attempts to define what are sometimes called 'absolute truths'. Yet people can and do say with certainty and with **right** on their side that, as it was put in the American Declaration of Independence, 'we hold these truths to be self-evident'. Determining and revering what is true must be close to the heart of educational life, just as it is to making sense of life itself long after one leaves the classroom. Plato, as is well known, appointed as his trinity of educational **values**, truth, **beauty** and goodness, and even a very little philosophic debate will quickly lead people to see how intertwined these supreme values are, how beautiful truth is, how being a good person is inseparable from being a truthful person, and how goodness itself (the goodness, say, of unselfish devotion, or the goodness of a beautiful building) is at once radiant and indisputable, possessing, that is, both truth and beauty.

Yet plenty of objections may be made to putting things so confidently. At a time when, for worse and for better, truth is assailed by relativism, or the argument that since all claims about truth are peculiar (relative) to time and place, truth is either uncertifiable or merely 'true for' you, me, or other persons and places. There are then two kinds of relativist. The first makes it relative to say what it is rational to hold true, or to believe. Thus, the fourteenth-century astronomer rationally held it to be true that the sun moved round the Earth. That astronomer was wrong but rational. The second, the hard relativist, claims however that the fourteenth-century astronomer's belief was true then, but isn't now. This is surely extreme.

Relativism has had a long run for its money once historians and anthropologists began to discover just how various and contradictory were and are the claims to truth which human beings could make about the world. At the same time, scientists and philosophers were coming to the conclusion that in spite of all its successes, science itself could not mirror a perfectly clear reflection of how nature worked, and would have to acknowledge the shakiness of **knowledge** itself, the historical changefulness of the 'absolute presuppositions' which comprised the frameworks of thought.

This led one **school** of American thinkers styling themselves 'pragmatists' to think of truth not as something clear and fixed, but merely as the circumstances of 'warranted assertability'. Not only for the pragmatists, but for all theories of truth, however, it seems plausible to distinguish between 'correspondence theories' and 'coherence theories', and to demand of any claims to truth that they square up sufficiently with both. According to the first, a statement or proposition is true only if it *corresponds* with the facts (although of course a statement may seem so to correspond and still be false; this is very much at issue in religious claims to truth). According to the second, statements are true insofar as they are *coherent*, that is, insofar as they match due criteria of consistency, evidence, logic and **authority**.

The English philosopher J. L. Austin said that 'the **theory** of truth is a series of truisms' and this truth should reassure us when the relativists get busy. For there is surely no difficulty at all in our agreeing that *truthfulness* is both a central value in education and an essential attribute of every educator. Trust on the part of the student in the teacher's truthfulness is the currency of all classroom exchanges, as it is the political currency of a free **society**. Politicians may have to lie from time to time, but only tyrannies can be based on lies. The expectations of truthfulness on the part of the rulers is the guarantee of a **democracy** and that expectation must be taught and learned at **school**.

FURTHER READING

J. L. Austin (1961), 'Truth', in *Philosophical Papers*. Oxford: Oxford University Press.
Wilf Carr and S. Kemmis (1986), *Becoming Critical: Education Knowledge and Action Research*. London: Falmer Press.
Peter Horwich (1990), *Truth*. Oxford: Oxford University Press.
Richard Rorty (1998), *Truth and Progress*. Harmondsworth: Penguin.
Bernard Williams (2002), *Truth and Truthfulness*. Princeton: Princeton University Press.

truth

Understanding

The first thing to understand about human understanding is just how wide is its reach and penetrative its insight. Saying this is saying much of what is set out in the entry on **mind**. Our understanding moves towards its goal as a **person** moves from darkness to light. These are the metaphors we naturally use when describing how we come to understanding. The twentieth-century German philosopher, Martin Heidegger, wrote:

> Only by **virtue** of light, i.e. through brightness, can what shines show itself, that is, radiate. But brightness in turn rests upon something open, something free … where one being mirrors itself in another speculatively – there openness … the free region is in play. Only this openness grants to the movement of speculative **thinking** the passage through what it thinks. (P. 384)

It seems natural to understand understanding by way of metaphors of enlightenment, and of moving from thickets and enclosures to clearings and sunshine. The compulsion to understand is unstoppable and ubiquitous. Humans seek, with notable success, to understand and depict one another, to pursue inquiry into the vastness of the universe, to repair creation and achieve destruction. One interminable debate turns upon whether there are ultimate limits to human understanding – whether, that is, there are things which in **principle** we cannot of their nature understand and, indeed, whether – as the eleventh-century theologian St Anselm put it, 'I believe that I may understand' – whether, that is, beliefs necessarily precede understanding, anyway of such giant topics as god or genetics.

In the smaller confines of **pedagogy**, it seems to be the case that teachers are trapped by certain clichés about what understanding, in relation to consciousness and experience, consists in. The philosopher Wittgenstein, though always difficult to follow, is a wonderful guide – when understood – to understanding. He says:

> Try not to think of understanding as a 'mental process' at all. For *that* is the expression which confuses you. But ask yourself: in what sort of case, in what kind of circumstances, do we say, 'Now I know how to go on' when, that is, the formula *has* occurred to me. (Wittgenstein, 1953)

Wittgenstein tells us that we grasp something as intelligible according to particular *circumstances,* and those are what we think of when describing the **experience** of understanding. His test case is of what it means to say someone understands what they are reading. The change when a pupil begins to read with understanding is a change in **behaviour,** and he asks if someone is reading the numbers when looking at a clock. No, of course not; the person is telling the time.

The moral of all this is to think of understanding not as a psychological **question** but as **learning** how to *do* something. When trying to say what understanding is (and to recognise when it happens), therefore, avoid attempts to psychologise and avoid also **standard** clichés, about reading for example, such as 'shouting at print'. Instead, take care to describe as common-sensibly as possible *what actually happens* when we can say, of ourselves or of our student, 'Now we know how to go on'.

FURTHER READING

R. G. Collingwood (1945), *The Idea of Nature.* Oxford: Oxford University Press.

D. W. Hamlyn (1978), *Experience and the Growth of Understanding.* London: Routledge and Kegan Paul.

Stuart Hampshire (1959), *Thought and Action.* London: Chatto and Windus.

Martin Heidegger (1979), *Basic Writings,* edited by David Krell. London: Routledge and Kegan Paul.

Ludwig Wittgenstein (1953), *Philosophical Investigations,* para 154. Oxford: Basil Blackwell.

understanding

A 'value' is a fierce little condensation of meaning, which is to say something the associations and realisations of which matter significantly to a **person**, and command, to a greater or lesser degree, his or her allegiance. Value is, therefore, the generalising term for all such meanings, and invoked and respected as marking out the large field of abstract **qualities** grounded in concrete **experiences** which we have learned to cherish and foster, to teach as admirable to our children and, in many cases, to protect and impose by **tradition** and by law. All forms of conduct or articles produced which a people ratifies and admires, commends and perpetuates, enshrine and enact values.

Values may obviously be very much at odds, not alone as between **societies** of differing geography or history, but within the one society, as when for example the demands of **equality** collide with those of liberty, or when the strong value all societies put on the home and the strong sense of belonging which it naturally engenders conflict with the value ascribed to the independence and self-reliance sought by children and bestowed by parents.

It is not easy always to determine why human beings value what they do, nor to distinguish between valuing things because we cherish them, nor cherishing things because they are valuable. A vigorous convention in the everyday view of values which has deep roots in educational **theory** is to make a sharp distinction between facts as being **objective** and observable, and values as being subjective and inward. But this distinction is hard to maintain. The very meaning of factually descriptive terms may carry an evaluative charge. Thus, 'poisonous' is a factual description of the properties of a given mushroom but it also has a rather plain evaluative content.

Some philosophers, moreover, have concluded that to apply any evaluative **language** correctly and according to the rules for its application is indeed to be identifying the moral facts objectively because according to the rules for using such terms. Others suggest that in **questions** of value, 'subjective' and 'objective' be dropped altogether, and 'intersubjective' always used instead of either.

Obviously 'value' is also used of arithmetical results, but this is a different sense as in 'the value of this equation is ...'. Nonetheless much effort has been expended on finding numerical equivalents for value decisions, the greatest successes coming not from intrinsic valuations but 'ordinal' ones, that is numerical values calculated against a ranking of value preferences in a statistically selected population.

The very idea of value is much influenced by **professional** valuers whose **authority** is important in the maintenance of values in what may usefully be seen as a competing market. Such valuers not only include those whose job title announces this function, as in the case of property or jewellery valuers, but also those teachers in **schools** and universities whose profession it is to ascribe and give authority to the valuations implicit in, say, the **disciplines** of **art**, literature, music, let alone history or politics.

The word is also used in a strictly technical sense when measuring school success. Schools must now pay attention to their results in relation to 'value-added' scores. These are measured according to the difference between the results predicted for a particular cohort of pupils (based on their prior attainment), and the results they actually gained. If they did better than expected, then the school 'added value'. If they did worse, then the value-added score is negative. In some calculations, a further factor is added based on the socio-economic situation of the pupils, and this is called the 'contextual value-added' score.

FURTHER READING

Marc Blaug (1985), *Economic Theory in Retrospect.* Cambridge: Cambridge University Press.

Malcolm Budd (1996), *Values of Art: Pictures, Poetry and Music.* Harmondsworth: Penguin.

James Laird (1929), *The Idea of Value.* Cambridge: Cambridge University Press.

Ludwig Wittgenstein (1966), *Lectures and Conversations on Aesthetics and Religious Belief.* Oxford: Blackwell.

value

Virtue as a term of moral approval or even as a goal of moral **development** is presently almost absent from official educational discourse although much debated in the strong revival of ethics as a topic in academic philosophy. In everyday conversation including the conversation of staffrooms, on the other hand, the names of the virtues remain in common use.

It is worth recalling from the outset that *virtu* in its etymological origins takes its root from the Latin for a man, *vir*, and that, therefore, the virtues were thought of by their first great codifier, Aristotle, as strictly masculine properties. All the same, any argument about the virtues (in his case always spoken of in the plural) must start from the Aristotelian view that **morality** cannot be ordered as a legislative system ('do your duty', 'keep your promises', 'be sensitive to others'), but rather that the virtues express the best natural traits in a **person**'s character, and that to be virtuous is to act from and upon those traits in the best way a given moral situation permits. The state of virtue is, for the Aristotelian, that condition of well-being (*eudaimonia*) in which one's best attributes find their best means of flourishing.

Thomas Aquinas, seeking to accommodate Christianity to classical texts, provided powerful justifications for the Catholic list of the cardinal virtues – prudence, **justice**, fortitude, temperance – while contriving a formidable apparatus for their being enacted in human life. His analysis of the human will, of intention, **choice**, reflection and deliberation, constituted the lasting matrix of virtuous thought and action, and survives today in ordinary moral parlance of all kinds (his enormous influence being extended to Islam by his admirer, Ibn Roshd).

This glimpse of early ethical **theory** must serve to indicate how present-day **education** can only comprehend the virtues as constituted historically by the many names seeking to describe and commend the good life. Perhaps the most powerful such figure in modernity was Immanuel Kant, writing at the high point of the Enlightenment in the late eighteenth century. He sliced away the **idea** of a canonical list of virtues, and turned the virtuous man or woman into a hero of conscience. Virtue was to repose in the **individual** of good will following the absolute injunction to treat other individuals only as ends and never as means. Every moral action was **subject** to the one interpretation, itself named by Kant 'the categorical imperative', that how one acts shall follow the maxim that anyone in these circumstances should act likewise.

Kant's revolutionary theory radically individualised ethics, and turned virtue into his abstract maxim. It handed over ethics to the liberals, and gave voice to the Romantic movement, with the passionate permissions it gave to individuality. In the almost 200 years since he wrote, educators have struggled to reconcile individual ethics and the crux of choice with a non-dogmatic, much extended, but still cardinal list of the virtues.

Of late, they have been much helped by recent Aristotelians, notably Alasdair MacIntyre, who have written of each human life as a narrative of autobiography. The good life is then each individual's effort to make as truthful a **work** of **art** as possible out of the stuff of his or her living. This will be truthful in that it includes some chapters of which the author is ashamed but will not baulk at, and a work of art in that it takes on meaningful shape and presence, even **beauty** and **power**, as it progresses. It can then only be known as a life one might be proud of, shaped by those virtues of which one was capable, after death, and in a secular **society** this must do for immortality.

By and large, teachers are queasy in speaking readily of the virtues, unless they help themselves from a formal religion. Yet a pupil can make no future sense without some attempt to match a picture of a livable virtuous life to those dispositions truly to be found in his or her character. That this discovery reaches well beyond the pious, timid limits of personal and social education into the practical rationalities and **culture** of the **school** should go without saying.

FURTHER READING

Zygmunt Bauman (1993), *Post-Modern Ethics*. Oxford: Blackwell.

Sissela Bok (1978), *Lying: Moral Choice in Public and Private Life*. Brighton: Harvester Press.

Phillipa Foot (1978), *Virtues and Vices*. Berkeley: University of California Press.

Alasdair MacIntyre (1981), *After Virtue*. London: Duckworth.

Mary Midgley (1984), *Wickedness: A Philosophical Essay*. London: Routledge and Kegan Paul.

Judith N. Shklar (1984), *Ordinary Vices*. Cambridge, MA: Harvard University Press.

virtue

Vocation

The word 'vocation' comes from the Latin *vocare*, to call, and originally it meant a religious calling. Over time, it came to mean a calling to other professions, usually of a socially worthy kind, for example, being a doctor might be called a vocation, or a teacher. It's unlikely that anyone would say 'I have a vocation to be a city banker'.

In **schools**, the word is generally used as an adjective, 'vocational', to describe anything that is to do with the world of **work**. 'Work-related learning' is part of the National Curriculum and is an entitlement for all pupils. Schools also offer vocational **subjects** at Key Stage 4. Students can opt to take vocational subjects at GCSE or A level, or national vocational qualifications (NVQ). These are meant to lead directly into certain types of work, for example, engineering, health and social care. It is important that schools and post-16 providers offer these courses, as they help to fulfil one of the 'five outcomes' for children and young people – achieving economic well-being.

As an adjective, the word seems to mean a preparation for work, or for a specific job. As a noun, 'vocation' still retains a sense of dedication to one's work.

FURTHER READING

www.vocationallearning.org.uk

Wisdom

'Wisdom' is a word rarely uttered in professional or official educational discourse. Anglo-Saxon in origin, it was already well established prior to the great melting pot of the Renaissance that gave us so many of the words and meanings that now frame our **understanding** of what constitutes **education**. Conceptually, wisdom is closely related to **experience**. In its primary sense 'wisdom' denotes the **knowledge** that comes with experience and is consequently often associated with age and the process of ageing: 'thou shouldst not have been old before though wast wise', the Fool tells Lear. To be wise is to have sound **judgement** and discernment. It involves a judicious application of experience and of the knowledge gained through experience: precisely what Lear, in his 'foolish' renunciation of **responsibility**, lacked in his descent into the great furnace of doubt.

Wisdom, then, is one of the gifts that more experienced learners may pass on to less experienced learners. In that sense, wisdom is an indispensable attribute of the educator, whose job it is not only to impart knowledge and understanding but also guidance as to how such knowledge and understanding might be applied. However, wisdom may also be oppressive, precisely because it is difficult to challenge. Its **authority** is based on the often unverifiable past experience of those who are deemed to be 'older and wiser'. An over-reliance on wisdom may therefore be interpreted as authoritarian or paternalistic. Learners need to acquire their own wisdom rather than have the wisdom of others thrust upon them. Wisdom dictates that we are discerning and circumspect with regard to what wisdom we impart and to whom and under what circumstances we impart it.

It is also worth bearing in mind that relatively young persons may be in possession of a wisdom denied to their elders. They may have had experiences, and derived a wisdom from those experiences, that are beyond the ken of an older generation. The phrase 'street-wise' captures one aspect of a kind of wisdom that some young people may have had to acquire in certain type of settings. But young people may also have experienced anguish and loss that are unknown and unknowable to the elders who have educational responsibility for them. If wisdom is derived from experience, then it is important to acknowledge that experience is extremely varied and that on occasion, the experience of young people has lessons for the old.

There is a further line of thought which is highly relevant to any consideration of the **concept** of wisdom. Notwithstanding the contribution of the Romantic movement in realigning knowledge with experience, knowledge has, since the Enlightenment, become increasingly divorced from the experiential resources of wisdom. Knowledge has become associated with a particular mode of scientific inquiry, whereby experience becomes both marginalised and objectified. One of the more interesting **developments** associated with post-structuralism is the attempt to reintroduce the **idea** of the knowing **subject** into informed discussions of what constitutes knowledge and of how knowledge relates to everyday experience. The **concept** of wisdom is crucial to these emergent understandings precisely because it reinstates the experiential.

FURTHER READING

R. Barnett (1994), *The Limits of Competence: Knowledge, Higher Education and Society*. Buckingham: Society for Research into Higher Education and Open University Press.
N. Maxwell (1987), *From Knowledge to Wisdom*. Oxford: Blackwell.
Mary Midgley (1989), *Wisdom, Information and Wonder: What is Knowledge For?* London: Routledge.

key concepts in education

Work

Work, the simplest, most all-encompassing **value** in our **society** has, as one would expect, a large and pervasive realm both in the ethics of daily **school** life, and in the specific zones of the **curriculum**. If, as suggested, the curriculum is thought of as distributed across the five main such 'zones of value' in our **culture** – the realms of nature and the globe, the significance of death, the meaning of the past, the more personal values of domestic life and the importance of work – then this last, *work*, covers both the 'instrumental' (that is, practical, purposeful, necessary to all aspects of common life) and the 'significant' (that is, as giving meaning beyond the practical) activities of **education**.

Portioning out work and leisure is taken for granted from the earliest days in the primary school. The hard and serious **subjects** are dealt with in the morning, the lighter ones in the afternoon as children tire; Friday afternoons, leading into the leisure time of the weekend, are often reserved for the special **interests** chosen by the pupils ('What's this afternoon?' a nine-year-old asked; 'Interests? Oh, they're so boring').

Thus work is marked off from play, in education and everywhere else. The poet Philip Larkin begins his poem *Toads*:

> Why should I let the toad *work*
> Squat on my life?

and those lines catch the resentment everyone feels at some time at the sheer necessity and drudgery of having to work, to turn out early on a wet morning and not be home until after dark. At the same time, not to have work, to be unemployed, is to be deprived of social meaning and placed in temporary suspense, awaiting return to the normality of work, and, therefore, recognised by the officers of state as a taxable participant in the urgent business of producing-and-consuming.

Ever since the revolutionary ideals of **freedom** and **equality** roused people to the idea of deliberative historical change, there have been political movements and thinkers seeking a way to make work absorbing and interesting to as many workers as possible. In the mid-nineteenth century, William Morris, at his factory and in his writing, and John Ruskin in his movement for working men, the Guild of St George, argued passionately for devising ways to make work more like **art**. Seeing that work was the defining activity of an **individual** and a social **class**, they struggled, along with the early trade unions, either to make work more fulfilling or, where that was impossible, to reduce the hours spent doing it and correspondingly to increase the pay for doing it.

This was the historical process which, for Karl Marx, became 'the class struggle'. Nowadays, the political aspect of the reform of work has leaked away, but the struggle to lighten its burden goes on. The very nature of industrial production and the drive to maximise capital accumulation led straight to the repetitious, reductive steps of mass assembly. Craft vanished, to be replaced by minute **technique**. The coming of the computer reduced human intervention and practical variety even more. The scope for creative and purposeful labour shrank to a minimum.

For a while, it seemed that the new technologies would drastically reduce the amount of time everybody would have to spend at work, but this hope proved delusory and at present the British work longer hours than any other nation in the European Union. The so-called 'work–life balance' is a topic on the lips of all politicians, and an increasing (but still tiny) number of people who can afford it or who are prepared to lose salary either retire early or move out of intensive schedules into the freer and more creative timetables of 'alternative lifestyles', even of self-sufficient smallholdings.

One of the most important contributions to the **understanding** and undergoing of work has been the sustained creativity of teachers to make classroom life vitalising and gripping. Nor have they failed in this effort. For while a part of a school's duties is indeed to inculcate the larger **society**'s **principles** of hard work, punctuality, keeping-to-schedule, observation-of-proper-**standards**, the other, bigger part is to teach how to direct these **disciplines** (and even, in so doing, to subvert them) towards human fulfilment and happiness, and to the realisation of the common good.

FURTHER READING

Harry Braverman (1974), *Labour and Monopoly Capital: The Degradation of Work in the 20th Century*. New York: Monthly Review Press.

Manuel Castells (1996), *The Rise of the Network Society*. Oxford: Blackwell.

John Goldthorpe (1968), *The Affluent Worker: Industrial Attitudes and Behaviour*. Cambridge: Cambridge University Press.

Krishan Kumar (1995), *From Post-Industrial to Post-Modern Society*. Oxford: Blackwell.

Richard Sennett (1998), *The Corrosion of Character: Personal Consequences of Work in the New Capitalism*. New York: W. W. Norton.

Youth

'Youth's a stuff will not endure' wrote Shakespeare in one of his songs, and classical literature is loud with laments on the shortness of youth, as well as its blissful excesses, its passions (especially for love and sex), its recklessness, its gaiety and its giving itself to life and the moment. What is less celebrated in the poetry is also the general conviction of youth that it is always in the **right** and in any case justified in doing whatever it wants simply by **virtue** of being young. But whatever **judgements** we might come to about the general desirability of the young and the splendour of its enjoyments, the **concept** of youth is fairly bursting with contents from its cultural past.

As one would expect, the span of youth is nowhere precisely defined. **Childhood** for some centuries was thought of as terminating with puberty (marriages important to monarchies were usually settled by the age of 15 in Elizabethan times). By a later measure, childhood ended when young men could be conscripted to serve in wartime, the age for which was set (in 1915) at 18. By another token, universal suffrage was only reduced from 21 to 18 by the Labour Government of 1966–70.

All these manoeuvres turned around social uncertainty as to the point at which a child became … well, what? A youth? A young **person**? In 1882 the novelist Henry James wrote a novel entitled *The Awkward Age* about a girl becoming a young woman both suddenly and gradually, 'putting her hair up', leaving behind nursery tea for the adult dinner table, being proposed to, turning from innocence to **experience**.

These are 'the rites of passage' as the anthropologists call them, whereby an **individual** moves his or her status from child to adult. Until quite recently (and, for instance, in some African and Indonesian tribes, still) the rite in **question** was held to be so serious, for boys at least, that the mark of adulthood was scored into their skulls and incised in their cheeks with knives.

The category 'youth' has, therefore, a varied and sometimes fearful history, its advent shaped by ritual and its meanings muffled and secretive. In the past half-century or so, the category has, at the hands of consumerism taken on a new and momentous significance, as marking out a large and novel membership in the consumer marketplace. From about 1950 onwards, the school-leaving population was given access to employment with far greater **freedom** to spend on itself than ever before. Rising prosperity and a different evaluation placed on youthful independence gave young people (as the phrase became) spending power, a new kind of self-awareness and **identity**, a membership one of another and, also in a forceful way, a widespread opposition to the parent generation, a loosening of the hold of senior **authority**.

As heavy industry closed down under Mrs Thatcher in the 1980s, the old forms of apprenticeship, with their hard-handed **traditions** of subordination and **learning**, vanished. Much swifter mobility in search of work and money broke up long-standing neighbourhoods and all these submarine forces worked to confirm the membership of youth. Youth, in its turn, seized upon those glad tokens of its insuppressibility such as rock music and the weird attire found in clothes shops designed expressly to provide the young with a distinctive uniform. The machinery of celebrity, already functioning as a separate industry among those of the cultural media, instantaneously produced celebrities cut out specifically to act as emblems of what was accurately called 'youth **culture**' – a special set of conventions, customs, **principles** of social exchange, rituals and *patois* functioning to mark off youth from the rest of (malevolent and repressive) society.

Policy and politics had to make new accommodations for this teeming multitude. The assumption was made that its members could be left to depend on parental support for much longer than was the case when boys and girls left **school** and went straight to **work**. (The full benefits of the minimum wage are not paid until young people are in their mid-20s and not so young.) The National Youth Agency, along with diverse youth services provided by churches, associations such as Scouts and Guides, battle to create space, refuge, kindly and bureaucratic support for this vast, uncitizened, generally boisterous, sometimes brutal constituency. It is economically important yet socially functionless. It makes people afraid, it is vilified in the press; it is afflicted by monstrous boredom; it is widely believed to be drunk or drugged every Friday; it is largely populated by decent, hopeful, friendly and open-minded people looking for the usual components of the good-enough life: their own home, a sufficient job, others to love, a handsome town to live in, transport to get about in, an honest government … this is the story to be put together and told by an **education** system which can stand up to such a task.

FURTHER READING

Martin Amis (1986), *The Moronic Inferno*. Harmondsworth: Penguin.
Bob Dylan, (2004), *Chronicles I*, New York: Simon and Schuster.
Eric Erikson (1968), *Identity: Youth and the Social Crisis*. New York: Random House.
Simon Firth (1978), *The Sociology of Rock*. London: Constable.
Norman Mailer (1968), *The Armies of the Night*. London: Weidenfeld and Nicolson.
Tom Wolfe (1972), *The Kandy-Kolored Tangerine Flake Streamline Baby*. London: Granada.

key concepts in education